Lisbon.

After several lost decades the Portuguese capital has woken from its slumber. One of the fastest-changing cities in Europe, Lisbon sits at the sweet spot of transformation as new businesses and creative pioneers look to shape its future.

Portugal's colonial past has become a vibrant, multi-cultural present, with a diversity of art and music alive in its streets and manifold cuisines. The Atlantic on the doorstep provides the freshest seafood and allows for a short beach break—this is the only European capital where girls and boys take their surfboards on the metro. Water, sun and its famous light are the city's key ingredients.

In Lisbon, LOST iN spoke to a musician who's packed stadiums with modern interpretations of African dance beats, a food expert who knows every table, an innovative fashion designer, a singer bringing fado to the new generation, a multifaceted writer and a local artist couple. It's all about original minds and the creative vibe. Get lost in the sights, sounds and flavours of the city. Get lost in Lisbon.

GW00497869

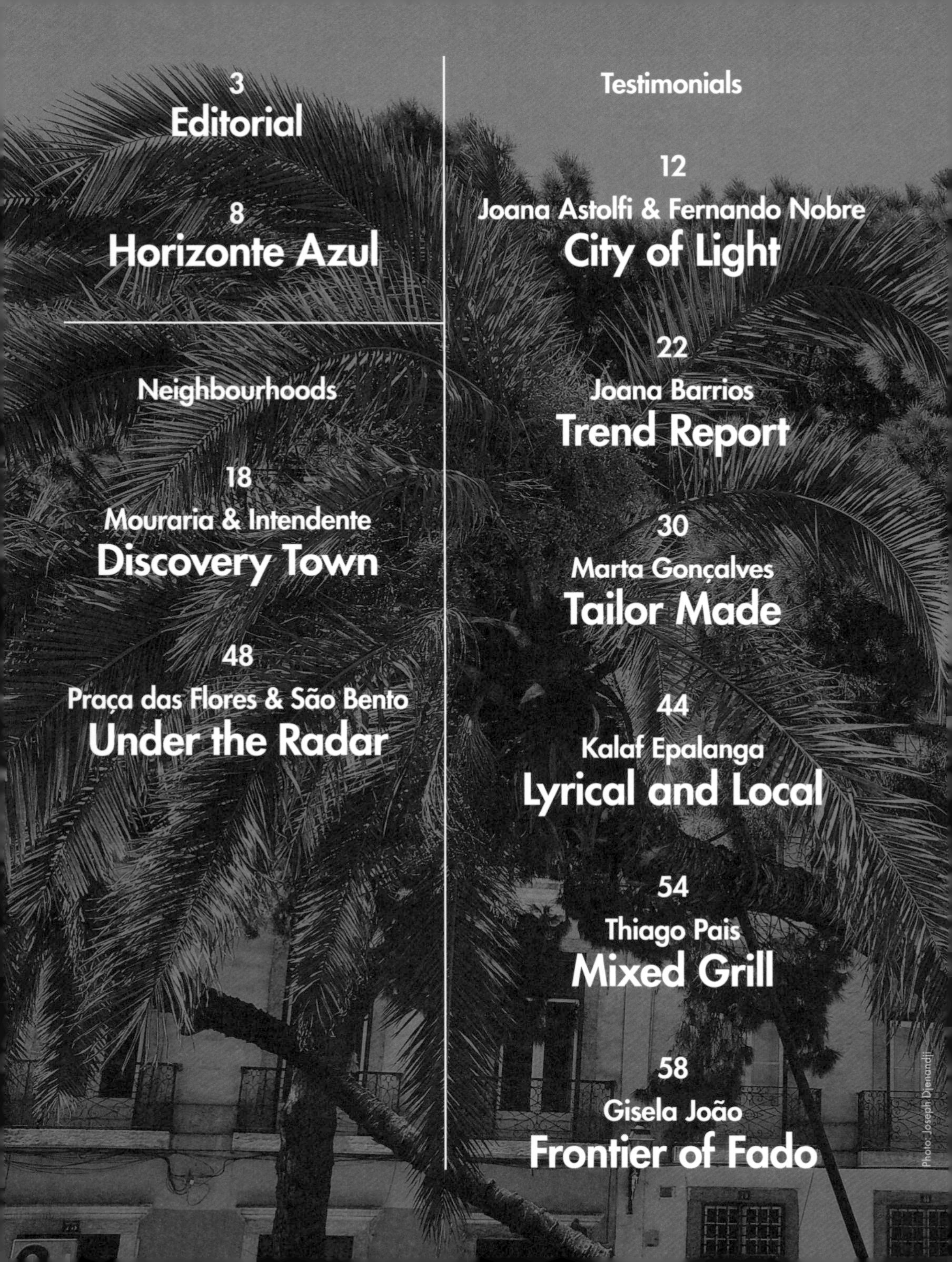

3
Editorial

8
Horizonte Azul

Neighbourhoods

18
Mouraria & Intendente
Discovery Town

48
Praça das Flores & São Bento
Under the Radar

Testimonials

12
Joana Astolfi & Fernando Nobre
City of Light

22
Joana Barrios
Trend Report

30
Marta Gonçalves
Tailor Made

44
Kalaf Epalanga
Lyrical and Local

54
Thiago Pais
Mixed Grill

58
Gisela João
Frontier of Fado

Photo: Joseph Djenandji

Story

26
One Night in the Village
João Ferreira Oliveira

64
O Sapato
Gonçalo M. Tavares

Showcase

34
Entre Nós
Pauliana Valente Pimentel

62
Editors' Picks
Bugigangas

64
Index

Lisbon life has always been intertwined with its waterways, and the *Espaço Espelho d'Agua* ("mirror of water" space) reflects the currents of its history. In 1940 the Exhibition of the Portuguese World was a pomp project by the Estado Novo dictatorship—the Espaço was built to be its beer hall, placed symbolically where the conquistadores had set sail five centuries before on their mission to dominate the world. In 2014, it reopened after careful renovation as an arts and

cultural centre. It even contains a business incubator, representing Lisbon's reinvention as a startup node. The service and food at its café-restaurant might have mixed reviews; but the crisp modernist architecture, interior vertical gardens and shimmering views of the River Tagus are truly transcendental.
• Espaço Espelho D'Água, Avenida Brasília, 210, Belém

Sound of Saudade

Fado music might be the classic Lisbon soundtrack, but touristy experiences are to be avoided. Locals might suggest cosy *Tasca Bela* instead, where Bela's daughters make you feel at home. Among the tapas-like "petiscos", try the "chouriço assado", a blood sausage cooked at the table (pictured). The atmosphere is relaxed and casual but at 10pm, show-time, the rule is clear: silence. Give in to elegant guitars and melancholic voices singing poems of love and tragedy. Even non-lusophones will end up humming along with the locals. Book ahead.
• Tasca Bela, Rua dos Remédios, 190, Alfama

From Art-filled Parks to Historical Bars

Horizonte Azul

African Night Flight

In a city with such a heavy influx of African culture, dedicate an evening to reverse musical colonialism. *B.Leza* (São Paulo) is a Lisbon staple for touring African bands, with a jam-packed programme that sees it open five days a week. Continue your exploration at thumping *Discoteca Luanda* (Estrela), where things ramp up after 3am thanks to regional live acts and DJs with a penchant for reworked Afro rhythms. Discover what kizomba and kuduro are all about by getting down with the city's diehard fans.
• Various locations, see Index p. 64

Outdoors · Food | **A Change of Perspective**

Lisbon's seven hills are dotted with spots for panoramic views, but for a sundowner in sight of the city's beautiful riverfront, you'll have to cross the Tagus. Take the orange Cacilheiros ferry ten minutes from Lisbon's Cais do Sodré station to Cacilhas in Almada. Despite the city's long heritage as a Moorish stronghold, today it's just a dense urbanisation in Lisbon's shadow. On arrival, turn right and follow the river path. Inhale, exhale, and take in the remains of the national shipbuilding industry before investors tear it all down for the luxury condos of "Lisboa South Bay". You're just in time, then, to visit *Restaurante Ponto Final*. Right on the river, it offers a solid Portuguese kitchen and spectacular views. If your palate craves crab, fish or "percebes" (a local barnacle variety), try *Cabrinha I* by the ferry terminal. This neon-lit, wood-paneled "marisqueira" offers fresh seafood, helpful waiters and an easy, residential vibe.

• Almada, various locations, see Index p. 64

Culture | Treasured Grounds

One of the 20th century's wealthiest men, Armenian oil magnate Calouste Gulbenkian, spent 40 years gathering an astonishing art collection, and bequeathed it to his adopted home Portugal. The *Calouste Gulbenkian Museum*'s selection ranges from East to West, and from antiquity to the Old Masters and Impressionists. For a more local flavour, the Modern Art Centre can be found just opposite. Also belonging to the Gulbenkian Foundation, it was opened in 1983 to feature modern and contemporary Portuguese art, with some international works thrown in. Both museums are to be found in a stunning, expansive park, containing a rose garden, an open-air theatre, water gardens—and plenty more opportunities for serene inspiration. Look out for scultpures and installations among the landscaped grounds.
• Calouste Gulbenkian Museum & Gardens, Avenida de Berna, 45A, Avenidas Novas, museu.gulbenkian.pt

Night | Living History

Opened in 1936, *Gambrinus* has seen it all: clandestine lovers, conspiring spies, conferring politicians—these rooms breathe history. The interior has been the same since its 1964 remodelling—as have the red uniforms of the waiters. The quality of classics like "Sopa Rica de Peix" (fish stew) is as high as the prices. That's one reason down-to-earth Lisboners avoid the main room with its monumental granite fireplace. They'd go instead go for a beer and an affordable "prego" (steak sandwich) at the more informal bar.
• Gambrinus, Rua das Portas de Santo Antão 23, Pena, gambrinuslisboa.com

Outdoor | Hang Ten

Thirty minutes drive from Lisbon can be found romantic Sintra with its pastel palaces and green mountains and seaside Cascais with its jet-set vibe. But water sports lovers opt for *Praia do Guincho*—an Atlantic beach in a wild setting. There's a bus from Cascais train station—but don't forget your wet-suit as the water rarely tops 17 degrees, even in summer. The northern end is occupied by wind- and kite-surfers while the south is the terrain of regular surfers. A surf school, showers and beach-bars allow a full-day stay—make sure you eat at Bar do Guincho. If it all looks familiar—the spot was used in Bond's "On Her Majesty's Secret Service"—plus indie surfer flick "This Side of Resurrection".
• Praia do Guincho, Costa de Estoril

Food | Trading Place

Markets are a good way to get under the skin of a city—and the *Mercado de Ourique* balances old school and innovative, gourmet and more humble snacks, Portuguese and international cuisine. Smaller and more local than the famous Mercado da Ribeira downtown, it is also a fine excuse for exploring the neighbourhood of Campo de Ourique. Formerly a focus for trade and hotbed of revolutionary activity, it's now one of Lisbon's desirable neighbourhoods with its historic cafés and lush gardens.
• Mercado de Campo de Ourique, R. Coelho da Rocha 104, Campo de Ourique, mercadodecampodeourique.pt

Joana Astolfi
& Fernando Nobre
Joana is a designer, architect,
artist, scenographer and
vintage collector. She lived
abroad for more than
ten years before deciding her
hometown Lisbon was the
place to open her studio.
Fernando is a musician, per-
former, stage director and
actor. He was born in
Mozambique and despite
coming to Lisbon aged nine,
feels his soul remains African.
Their life changed with
the arrival of baby girl Duna

Joana Astolfi & Fernando Nobre, Artist & Musician

City of Light

Lisbon's magic is in its light, its infinite horizon and the vantage points to be found on almost every corner. Passionate about their chosen home, Joana and Fernando discuss where to find good music, theatre and vintage, debate the merits of taverns, and glow about the city's unique charms

Feira da Ladra
Alfama

Cantinho do Vintage
Beato

Muito Muito
at Lx Factory
Estrela

Møbler
Estrela

Belcanto
Baixa

Park
Estrela

Luvaria Ulisses
Baixa

Joana, how much of Lisbon's energy influences your work?

Joana: I was born in Lisbon and my father was born in Rio de Janeiro—he travelled the world and had many foreign friends. My house was always full of artists and architects. At 18, I left Portugal and lived away for 12 years in Munich, London, Los Angeles and Venice. After that, I wanted to go back to Lisbon to set up my studio. Why? Because Lisbon is the best city in the world, it's where I want to have my base and I prefer to work from inside out than the other way round. I cannot imagine living anywhere else, because of the pace of the city, the light, the food, the people, the endless views. All this is my motivation, my inspiration. There is one thing I really like to do, and it helps me relax—spending hours in vintage shops looking for objects with history I can add to my collection and use in my work.

What are your favourite places to look for vintage objects?

Fernando: The first time I met Joana was at the *Feira da Ladra*. I saw a beautiful woman walking there, with a glazed look, almost in a trance. And only six years later did we meet on the promenade of Largo Camões. A Cuban woman we both knew introduced us, and we've never let go of each other since.

Joana: Yes, wandering around the flea market—at Graça on Tuesdays and Saturdays—is one way for me to be alone. I hate to go there with people, I need to be focused in order to browse the stands. One of the places Fernando and I visit the most, however, is the *Cantinho do Vintage*, a large warehouse at Poço do Bispo. But there's more: the *Muito Muito at Lx Factory* in Alcantara, and for restored furniture, *Møbler* at Praça das Flores. Lisbon is a city with lots of history and I work a lot with history.

Where can we find some of your works?

Joana: Some of my installations are in the restaurants of chef José Avillez, like *Belcanto*. I also transformed two old 1950s Carris buses for the co-working project "Village Underground" at the Carris Museum. One bus is a coffee shop and the other a conference room. *Park*, a rooftop bar on the sixth floor of a car park, was made by me from scratch, from the garden to the wood.

You tend to focus on the 1940s–1960s. Is it possible to find remnants of that time in the city?

Joana: Very few, but there are still some shops that maintain traces. That's the case with *Luvaria Ulisses*, on Rua do Carmo, which is really worth a visit.

Joana, one of your famous creations are the iShells, headphones with seashells for earphones. Where is the best seaside place to wear them?

Joana: I need to reload my energies near the sea. I grew up in Cascais and so I go to the seaside at Guincho or Azenhas do Mar. But the iShells are actually a critique of the iGeneration who can't put down their devices. The idea is to use them in the midst of the hubbub of the city, so they can replace the calm feeling the sea imparts when you can't be near it.

Fernando, you were born in Mozambique and your parents are from Cape Verde. Where in Lisbon can we experience that cultural heritage?

Fernando: Lisbon is the capital of a more African Europe. When walking around, the cars that pass you at high speed with loud music are listening to kizomba or kuduro. You can feel Africa and be happy

Lisbon's fresh fish makes for excellent sushi, as you can discover at Japanese restaurant Tasca Kome

B.Leza
São Paulo

Casa Independente
Intendente

Tasca Kome
Baixa

MusicBox
São Paulo

LuxFrágil
Alfama

Azenhas do Mar
Odemira

Restaurante Adraga
Colares

Taberna da Rua das Flores
Bairro Alto

at *B.leza*, a bar/nightclub in Cais do Sodré, where many Angolans go to dance. The aforementioned Park, on a car park in Calçada do Combro, plays massive hip hop with African influences. Also at *Casa Independente*—a place we go to a lot—there is music of African origin. For example the resident band Fogo-Fogo play Cape Verdean music. What's interesting to note is that colonisation, which for me was traumatic, seems to be extinct in the capital, which already accepts Africans today— although there is still some "eye rolling". In my various musical projects, I go for funk and soul, but what I do in my solo project is to sing in creole and Portuguese.

If you had to take a tourist friend to three must-go places, which would they be?

Fernando: For dinner? *Tasca Kome*. To have a drink? Park. To dance? *MusicBox*, *LuxFrágil* or *B.leza*.

Joana: Tasca Kome? I don't agree. We wouldn't take someone to a Japanese restaurant. I'd take him to a fish and seafood restaurant by the sea, like *Azenhas do Mar* or *Restaurante Adraga*. I wouldn't go to Ramiro like everyone else, I also wouldn't go to Gambrinus to eat a "prego" (steak sandwich).

Fernando: Joana doesn't like going to "tascas" (taverns).

Joana: That's true, but I like *Taberna da Rua das Flores* where you can eat good Portuguese food. I take people there. I also show them the *Calouste Gulbenkian Museum*. I love the building, I love the gardens. I want to be buried there.

Calouste
Gulbenkian Museum
& Gardens
Avenidas Novas

Casa da Índia
Baixa

Lisbon Oceanarium
Parque das Nações

Museu Coleção
Berardo
Belém

Botanical Garden
Belém

In Bocca al Lupo
Principe Real

Culturgest
Areeiro

Primeiros Sintomas
São Paulo

Rua das Gaivotas 6
São Paulo

Chapitô
Alfama

Tokyo
São Paulo

So Fernando, you do like tascas. What's your favourite and what should be eaten there?

Fried baby horse mackerel with tomato rice or cockle rice at *Casa da Índia* in Chiado.

Joana: I wouldn't go there if they paid me. The only tasca for me is Das Flores.

Regarding child-friendly places, where would you go with your baby girl Duna?

Joana: Again, the Gulbenkian gardens, we go there constantly because Duna loves to feed the ducks. She also goes to Príncipe Real almost every day, sometimes to the *Oceanarium* or the *Museu Coleção Berardo*.

Fernando: the *Botanical Garden* is also great because of the butterflies.

Joana: Now she's almost two, she's beginning to be good company for dinner. We often go to the organic pizzeria *In Bocca al Lupo*.

Fernando, as a drama teacher, actor and director, which are the best theatres to visit?

I'm not just connected to the theatre, but also the performance. Therefore I think the *Culturgest* is always a good option because it brings the best theatre companies in a low-budget version. With regard to national theatres, I like the Teatro Nacional D. Maria II, which has undergone a revolution with the new director, and always has interesting events programmes. At Cais do Sodré there's the Primeiros Sintomas, a theatre group putting on new versions of classical plays, and a bit further on, on Rua da Boavista, there is the *Rua das Gaivotas 6*, with a theatre company made up of exclusively African actors. I have to mention *Chapitô*, where I teach, which has done some fantastic

social work, giving new opportunities to people with troubled lives.

And what about music?

There aren't many live music venues, but you can still see some bands in *Tokyo* and Musicbox, where my band Cais do Sodré Funk Connection were residents for a long time. LuxFrágil, the main nightclub in Lisbon, has a more mainstream offering—it's more concerned with the style and concept. Lisbon greatly influences the music I make—funk, for example, is more like dance with jazz origins, which can only succeed in a place where different cultures intersect, like here. Funk is dirty, it's sinful, it's life—and Lisbon is buzzing with all that. It makes sense to play outdoors with the sun and the heat, and party at an event like "Out Jazz", for example, where I've played. During summer these happen every weekend in various parts of the city.

What does Lisbon have that you can't find anywhere else in the world?

Fernando: It's a village, the light is fantastic and the food is wonderful.

Joana: The light, yes. And the immensity of the coast. It's unique and changes from kilometre to kilometre.

Fernando: You can go around Lisbon from one end to the other for only 10 euros by taxi. And eat well for five.

Joana: Human warmth. We are great hosts.

Fernando: The party lasts until sunrise.

Joana: No. It's the light. You have to experience it, it's inexplicable.

Founded by a visionary entrepreneur in 1925, Luvaria Ulisses is Portugal's last store totally dedicated to gloves

Discovery Town

Originally a refuge for the Moors, these narrow, sun-starved streets were a ghetto for centuries. But recent urban revitalisation has created one of Lisbon's most buzzing areas

Food Cultural Crossroad

Intendente's recent rehabilitation has transformed formerly notorious Rua do Benformoso into a rich multicultural hub. Alongside 500 metres of dilapidated buildings, where waves of immigrants have set up shop and home since the 1980s, it's now possible to taste the world. Among the Bangladeshi and Indian kitchens at no. 222 is *Dhaka* (Intendente), where the regulars eat the excellent biryani with their hands. Though the hidden Chinese eateries here are technically illegal, you're likely to eat beside a police officer, so don't worry—the one at *No. 43, 2nd floor* (Mouraria) is

a star for its crunchy aubergine with sweet and sour sauce. And at no. 76, the spicy soup at Vietnamese restaurant *Pho-Pu* (Mouraria) is among the best in town. Meanwhile, colourful Asian food markets serve up all manner of raw ingredients, tailors offer Mozambican capulana sarongs and retail warehouses stand beside traditional cultural associations. One such, at no. 244, is *Casa dos Amigos do Minho* (Intendente), where you can sample northern Portuguese foods and drink a strong "bagaço"—to round off your global tour back where you started.

• Various locations, see Index p. 64

Atop a hill, inside a theatre… Even few Lisboners know this spot. But the view that soars from here over Mouraria's rooftops is unparalleled. At *Café da Garagem*, visitors are invited to relax in front of the huge window with free binoculars, and enjoy a glass of red wine or a piece of chocolate cake. The retro décor is full of details such as tables made of old doors and vintage lamps, all accompanied by a diverse music selection. Don't forget to visit the theatre in the same building and check out the art exhibits on the top floor.
• Café da Garagem, Costa do Castelo, 75, Mouraria, teatrodagaragem.com

Food | Down to Earth

It only serves lunch and it's likely to be packed—but it's well worth the wait. In the heart of Mouraria, *Zé da Mouraria* is not only one of the most charismatic restaurants in the area. It's also a great example of how tasty and diverse traditional Portuguese gastronomy can be. Traditional decoration, affordable prices and huge portions have been its three commandments since opening doors in the 1990s. On Fridays and Saturdays go for the "bacalhau assado"—codfish grilled over a charcoal barbecue—a house specialty.
• Zé da Mouraria, Rua João do Outeiro, 24, Intendente

Shop | Retail Time Warp

Travel back several decades to an almost vanished way of life at *A Vida Portuguesa*. Among its charming 500 square metres at the flagship Intendente store are thousands of products, such as furniture, shoes, wine, pans, porcelain, soap and even bathtubs. Still produced today, these items have been around for decades, preserving their original retro design and brand image. As the owner explains, they "have been handed down through generations but still touch our hearts today". It's not a museum but it could easily be one.
• A Vida Portuguesa, Largo do Intendente Pina Manique, 23, Intendente, avidaportuguesa.com

Everybody's Table

Food is a universal language. For years, Adriana Freire dreamed of having an open kitchen full of people, with a big table where everybody could sit, eat and share. That dream finally came true in a converted garage in the heart of Mouraria. *Cozinha Popular da Mouraria* is a community kitchen offering daily meals and providing culinary training for underprivileged people. At the same time, "na cozinha" hosts thematic dinners and workshops, invites famous chefs to cook, provides catering and serves tasty lunches. Try it—it feels like visiting family abroad.
• Cozinha Popular da Mouraria, Rua das Olarias, 5, Mouraria, cozinhapopularmouraria.org

Culture Facing the Wall

"How can we keep a community's history alive?" British photographer Camilla Watson answered her own question in 2007 when she moved to Mouraria. Inspired by the generosity of the elderly living there, she made portraits of locals and printed them on wood, stone—and even walls. Called "A Tribute", this was her first outdoor exhibition and can now be seen next to her *Studio*. Now, you can also visit her second outdoor exhibition, "Retratos do Fado", images of revered fado musicians printed along the narrow streets, squares and alleys of Mouraria.
• Camilla Watson Studio, Largo dos Trigueiros, 16A, Mouraria, camillawatsonphotography.net

Shop Out on the Tiles

Joaquim José Cortiço was a well-known expert on buying and selling discontinued lines of the traditional tiles used to embellish Lisbon's build-ings. After he died in 2013, his grandchildren found an enormous collection of tiles encompass-ing more than 900 different patterns and styles, many unique and from factories no longer in business. To keep their grandfather's memory alive, they opened this store in 2014. While street vendors will often sell you tiles pried illegally from building façades, *Cortiço & Netos* is perhaps a better place to buy your tasteful slice of Lisbon.
• Cortiço & Netos, Calçada de Santo André, 66, Intendente, corticoenetos.com

Culture · Night | **Old School Independence**

Partying in this hood is an experience as diverse as its locals; offers range from African bars shaking to kizomba to DJs spinning atop fancy rooftops. But two key spots in particular have helped change Mouraria and Intendente's nightlife in recent years. *Casa Independente* was set up by two women who believed the area could transcend its troubled past. They transformed an old building into an open house with a weekly cultural agenda—and it was a hit. Inside is a large living room with tea and snacks at the cafeteria and comfy sofas in the backyard. A chill-out vibe reigns during the day; but at night Independente becomes a bar and disco with daily concerts, DJ sets, thematic parties and exhibitions.

Entrance is free. Meanwhile, at one of the most infamous crossroads in Mouraria, *Bar Anos 60* is an old-school pub. Despite its name, it was founded in the 1990s, and it's as messy as it is fun. And those Lisboners who were once afraid of setting foot in the area now pack it out every night. From jazz to Brazilian bossa nova, expect live concerts and jam sessions every weekend, cheap drinks, a dense cloud of cigar smoke and noisy locals dancing like crazy until 4am. If the door's closed, just ring the bell.

• Mouraria, various locations, see Index p. 64

Trend Report

Joana Barrios
She was inspired in 2008 by a Sonic Youth t-shirt to approach Lisbon's fetish theatre Teatro Praga, where she still works as an actress, writer and costume designer. She's collaborated with noted directors in Paris and Berlin and for three years was the ever-smiling bouncer at legendary club Lux/Frágil. Today, she runs an infamous blog called "Trashédia" and hosts the weekly TV show "Inferno"

The cultural emergence of Lisbon is well documented—as someone immersed in the vibrant fashion and theatre scene, Joana Barrios is well placed to give an insider view. She breaks down Portuguese fashion, tells us the talents to watch and informs on where to brush shoulders with the city's creative starlets

ComCor
Santo António

Slou
Bairro Alto

Sneak Peek
Baixa

It seems Lisbon is the new Berlin— the international crowd is discovering the city. Why now?

Some specialists are saying the boom of tourism in Portugal is happening right now because of the instability in countries like Greece or Turkey, two of the amazing destinations in the Mediterranean that have great people, amazing food, amazing weather and cheap prices. But that lost innocence, naïveté and coolness is just the simple way we've been living for ages now. Lisbon is also being wildly discovered and conquered because tourism is representing a key role in saving so many families from bankruptcy or expropriation. But still, I am very skeptical towards this kind of mass-market, low-cost tourism. It's weird, on the one hand, to be considered an exotic native in your home, and on the other it's bizarre to feel the city is gently kicking you out because your place could be making some foreigner happy. I lived the Barcelona catastrophic tourism model closely and I'd be really sad if the same happened to Lisbon.

Portuguese fashion is filling pages from "Vogue Italy" to the UK's "Times". Is there a renewal?

The fashion scene in Portugal is composed by designers, independent brands and industry. To get designer pieces as a consumer, you might have to visit designers' ateliers or a store called *ComCor*, where the owner Francisca Maltez has a selection of made-in-Portugal fashion. Independent brands either have pop-up stores or enroll in street markets and fairs where you can actually buy directly from the owners, which is very interesting and nice. Some independent brands benefit a lot from this because they grow a lot from small lucky strikes—when a piece

is worn by a celebrity or featured by a cool magazine or website or blog. Some brands have their own stores and manage to have great numbers. That's amazing, because they start as a small handcrafted idea and become strong brands. International attention is shaking things up, but there's still a lot to be done. Maybe that's why the fashion scene in Portugal is so exciting: there are so many job positions yet to be created, it's insane!

Who are the hot designers to watch?

Ricardo Preto, for his understanding of the female body and for this ability he has to produce exquisite designed pieces you can wear anytime, anywhere. Valentim Quaresma, whose exclusive jewellery pieces have been used by Lady Gaga; Vertty, a beach towel brand that's been selling worldwide for three years and growing every year; Estelita Mendonça, Pedro Pedro and Luis Carvalho. The great and unique Alexandra Moura. And La Paz, a Porto-born, super awesome brand that I buy and use like crazy, even though it's only for men. There's also two brands really worth watching: Baguera and Joana Mota Capitão, both in the jewellery business.

Where can we find fashion like that in Lisbon?

Apart from ComCor, I'd recommend *Slou* and *Sneak Peek*. If you want to go shopping in Lisbon the best area is around Baixa, Chiado and Príncipe Real, where you have the best selection of independent shops and brands.

Beyond fashion, in the other arts— are there other rising stars to put on the watchlist?

Young talents such as De Almeida e Silva, Diana Policarpo and Luís Lázaro Matos. For some

Rua das Gaviotas 6
São Paulo

Damas
Graça

Bar 49
Bairro Alto

Purex
Bairro Alto

LuxFrágil
Alfama

Cervejaria Ramiro
Intendente

amazing updates, there's Susana Pomba's blog missdove.org, a free guide covering all the exhibitions happening in the city, and her monthly "Old School" at *Rua das Gaivotas 6*. Please make sure you pay attention to João Pedro Vale and Nuno Alexandre Ferreira, Pedro Barateiro, Filipa César, Vasco Araújo and Gabriel Abrantes. And, of course, Teatro Praga.

Where does the creative scene meet?
I would say whenever there's an event at Rua das Gaivotas 6. Also at the bar *Damas*, at *Bar 49* right next to ZDB in Bairro Alto, *Purex*, and at the club *Lux/Frágil* in Santa Apolónia.

What is your favourite place in town?
The bathroom of Rua das Gaivotas 6.

As a creative personality, where do you get your inspiration?
Sometimes I can be creative, but most of the time I need to produce, and that's pretty nasty! I guess I go on collecting stuff in my mind, taking screenshots of things I see, taking notes the whole time, and keeping them safe, so when I need to create, I search through whatever I've collected. Most of the time I don't even know what I've written, and I get so frustrated! But most of all, I avoid driving and doing things that will prevent me from getting in touch with what surrounds me, because I really like to contemplate.

And how would you get lost in Lisbon? Take us on a walk.
So, I love the area of Martim Moniz and the whole Avenida Almirante Reis. It's just the most cosmopolitan area of the city, packed with people and shops and food and life. Before tourism, Lisbon had little to no movement on the streets, and this area would always be busy. The buildings are quite recent, some controversial squares and architecture can be found along the route that starts in Martim Moniz and ends in Areeiro. I like the differences and dichotomies and the notion of evolution you get if you tour it all the way up or down. Eat some seafood at *Ramiro* or enjoy a kebab in the many kebab corners available. Sink into those hostels and cheap hotels, skate the hall of Banco de Portugal, try to cross Praça do Chile without being hit by a car whether you're driving or walking.

Where have you always wanted to go in Lisbon and never made it?
They say there's an amazing steak in the most famous strip club, Elefante Branco. I'd love to taste that steak.

You travel a lot—what's missing in Lisbon?
So many things! Lisbon is an enchanting place precisely because of that, because there's a lot of potential and so little has yet been done. But right now I'd say it's missing great bistros with Portuguese-inspired food and some independent shops with good international brands.

Above: The events at Rua das Gaivotas 6 cross the boundaries between art, theatre, cinema and workshop
Below: Excellent seafood is on offer at Cervejaria Ramiro, where the initiated dine privately upstairs

One Night in the Village

João Ferreira Oliveira

For those from the countryside, everything's either very simple or very complicated. If it's complicated, it's too much bother—a certain level of organisation is needed to catalogue and feed the fears. That's why I chose from the start—for simplicity's sake—the traditional "go with the flow". Why waste beer money on a room when you can sleep on the street? That's what I thought about 20 years ago when I first came to Lisbon on my own...

Isaque and I, my childhood friend and neighbour were just passing, heading towards Alentejo, in the south, to go to a now famous rock festival that was then taking its first steps, just like us. We smoked and drank everything in our pockets, threw our sleeping bag on the floor of a tax office and slept like rocks until seven. We almost missed the bus. Normally we'd been woken up by the church bells or fireworks—not by the sound of a plane.

In Portuguese villages, at least in mine, there's not always bread, but every weekend there's fireworks. Because it's someone's birthday, because the son got into university, because the daughter finished her course, because someone recovered from illness, because there's a festival for Saint Whoever... All reasons are good enough to blow up the sky and express with gunpowder what can't be said with hugs.

If it were today, maybe we'd have kept drinking beer all night long. Where the bus station was before there's now a garden, the Blind Arch Garden, known for its 50-cent beers sought by students who shower the ground every other day with urine and fresh vomit to the chagrin of the residents. A neighbourhood gets so much younger and greener as the beer gets cheaper.

I came back to the city about five years later—having finished my studies in a country town—this time to work. I arrived by train in Santa Apolónia. The bus is a fine means of transport, but it's not ideal to keep using all your life. I think it was June, July, I don't remember; it was sunny and there weren't many people. There was a time when during summer there were few people in the city; now that time has gone, and the Lisboners who go away on holiday are replaced by foreign tourists coming on holiday—and yet it still continues to be a good season.

My whole future in front of me and just a backpack behind: the ideal load for discovering Lisbon. I went up to Graça, not knowing it was Graça, one of the oldest, most characteristic neighborhoods. I passed through the field of Santa Clara, where every Tuesday and Saturday is the Feira da Ladra flea market, but on that day, instead of junk, it was lined with jacarandá flowers that dyed the asphalt lilac, and I ended up sitting on a viewpoint watching the Tejo River.

It was strange, that I do remember very well. It was like I'd finally made it home. I called my parents saying I was at the hotel and they shouldn't worry, because within a week I'd have a permanent place. I hung up the phone and spent the night there, despite the wind. It's one of the windiest viewpoints and hence one of the city's least popular. There was a chapel behind me and the image of a saint—since I was little I've been afraid of saints, and still I did not feel cursed. In Portugal we can get rid of the fireworks and the church bell, but there's always a saint to light the way.

Years later, during one Eve of Saint Anthony, the patron saint of the city, and one of the most beautiful parties in the world, despite everything, especially the hangover and the smell of sardines that penetrates your blood forever, I fell asleep at the top of a viewpoint in Alfama and tumbled onto a roof. I survived with two scratches.

Even today, now I have more sense and only sleep on a bed or couch—sometimes not even there—like any responsible adult, I don't let a week go by without doing the rounds of the viewpoints and the old park benches. Some visit the astrologer, the witch or the doctor before making a big decision, I don't take a step without looking at the horizon. This is where I write most of my texts, if possible with a view of the 25 de Abril bridge in the background, "sitting in front of the endless blue of Lisbon", as Enrique Vila-Matas wrote in his book "Suicídios Exemplares" ("Exemplary Suicides")—a book of short stories in which an obsession with suicide drives the protagonists away from the temptation of death. One, "Morte por Saudade" ("Death by Saudade"), ends at a viewpoint of Lisbon, the one where I find myself writing these lines.

António Tabucchi, another writer, an Italian who fell in love with Fernando Pessoa and Portugal, who lived in Lisbon for many years, even told Vila-Matas the Portuguese capital has unique, beautiful and unusually dramatic places for committing suicide. I swore I wouldn't return to this topic, not only because it's sensitive, but because I thought I had exhausted all I had to say in a chronicle entitled "Como és bela e trágica Lisboa. Que nunca te vás abaixo com o peso dos turistas" ("How beautiful and tragic is Lisbon. May you never sink under the weight of the tourists"), written a few months ago on this same bench—but the will is stronger than common sense. It's an obsession. Not suicide, but this melancholy, crystal, incandescent light, this infinite blue that embraces the city.

I got lost, sorry. That's still happens here. Not as much as before, but it still happens. We run out of the house towards the grocery store—yes, there are still grocery stores—and we end up sitting to watch the river. We sit on a garden bench to plan the future and end up discussing the past. The famous "saudade", is that it? A feeling many Portuguese people like to call our own— granted that the expression can't be replicated in any other language.

Curiously, I felt the same in Istanbul, and I didn't even need to sleep on the street or sit on a bench—it was enough just to look at the Bosphorus. Just like Lisbon and Rome, old Constantinople also has seven hills. Does "saudade" travel with us or is it a burden lent by history and geography? Orhan Pamuk, man of the house and winner of the Nobel Prize for Literature in 2006, explains it all in the book "Istanbul: Memories and the City", in the chapter

"Hüzün-Mélancolie-Tristesse". Hüzün: a collective feeling that is to the Istanbul people what fado and saudade are to those of Lisbon.

Every time I go to the country, the few times I deem myself worthy enough to take the train to go to visit my family, my paternal grandfather—who's old but still has a good memory—asks me if I'm living in Graça yet. He knows I'm not. He was in the army there, more than 70 years ago. "Never liked Lisbon that much, but Graça was beautiful," he tells me. "It looked like a village."

Maybe that's the secret. Lisbon isn't really a city, but a set of little villages. Not neighbourhoods, all cities have those, but villages. The way in which the countryside continues to survive—sometimes to grow—between concrete avenues and cosmopolitan hotbeds continues to be remarkable. The majority of people from Lisbon, if not all of them, come from the countryside; they arrived on the same train I did, though with different needs. Many still keep, in their cupboards, a firework to launch the day they return home.

Maybe the whole country is a village and Lisbon the city that best represents "Portugality"—though without reflecting Portugal. No capital truly represents its country.

Much has changed since my grandfather's time, since my first night, and Lisbon seems to have definitively entered the world map of tourism. Yet, despite the mundane tics, it still retains its rural soul. Though it sometimes tries to extinguish it. The soul Gabriel García Marquez saw in 1975. A year after the revolution that took Portugal out of a 41-year dictatorship, the Colombian writer was among us to make a series of reports and to send a postcard to a friend, also a journalist, depicting the 25 de Abril bridge, on which he wrote "Lisbon is the biggest village in the world".

A village or an island, whatever. It's like any island—like a good book—when we look ahead we can see the past, the future, face our demons, and above all, return to the street of our childhood. Wherever that is.

João Ferreira Oliveira is a Portuguese journalist and writer, specialised in travel. In 2014 a road trip with two friends around the country resulted in the book "Around Portugal in 80 days". Their project "Grande Turismo" (www.grandeturismo.com) won the Portuguese blogger travel awards of 2016. He also writes children's books

Tailor Made

Marta Gonçalves
She's made a name for herself on the Portuguese fashion scene at just 24 years old. With Gonçalo Páscoa she founded innovative non-gendered fashion label HIBU, which she now runs alone, and has exhibited at Mode Lisboa, Bloom Portugal Fashion and London Fashion Week

With a production process rooted in a daily walk through the ancient streets of Alfama, Marta shares her method for integrating old Lisbon into her fashion, her pick of innovative design shops, an uncomplicated fado venue and the best value seafood around

Feira das Almas
Intendente

Calouste
Gulbenkian Museum
& Gardens
Avenidas Novas

Under the Cover
Avenidas Novas

Sunset Destination
Hostel
São Paulo

Are you originally from Lisbon?

I'm from the suburbs near Sintra, it's beautiful there. But I commuted to high school in Lisbon every day, to a school specialised in costume design. I wanted to make fashion, so I moved to Castelo Branco in the north to study fashion design. Then I returned to Lisbon where I met Gonçalo—my co-founder at HIBU, who recently left the brand.

Are your collections inspired by Lisbon, the country, the light?

I'm not sure if my work is influenced by the city. But the production process is adding to my creation: I'm working with a seamstress in Alfama, an area close to the city centre but also a bit apart. It's like old, traditional Lisbon. Every morning I walk there from Marquês de Pombal where I live. I walk along the Avenida de Liberdade, catch the new elevator up to Rua Santa Madalena, near the vantage point, and arrive in Alfama. The area feels "real". I like the people there. My seamstress is in her sixties and has all kinds of visitors. And everybody gives advice on my pieces, it's very funny! Part of my last collection was made from a painter's canvasses. All the people who came by told me if they didn't like it, or had ideas for improvements. It was charming and refreshing. We put the canvas in the street and painted it there —it was great to have an experience so related to Lisbon.

Your area Marquês de Pombal is not famous for being lively—is there a more creative part of the area?

I would say in Arroios, along Avenida Almirante Reis, between Anjos and Martim Moniz. You'll find a diverse population—many Indians and Pakistanis, which is rare in the city centre, and small

independent fashion shops and bars. Also once a month there's the *Feira das Almas*, a vintage market, where young creators sell. There are some nice food concepts though it's maybe a bit hipster. Another area being discovered by the creative class is Beato. There are industrial structures and a residential area, so it's perfect—only a bit difficult to reach by public transport.

Speaking of the creative scene, how are the prospects in Lisbon right now?

During the recession and with the austerity program it's been hard—everyone felt there were no prospects here. Now it's getting better—but slowly though. Maybe because the Portuguese are slow with our processes in a way. But we help each other to create and bring ideas to life—even if there's no budget.

Apart from your neighbourhood, which areas do you like?

As I mentioned, I love Alfama. But another place is the *Gulbenkian Gardens*—a park with interesting buildings, and a calm spot in the city. Next to the park is an amazing store for independent Portuguese and international magazines, *Under the Cover*. It's run by friends of mine, a doctor couple who run the business on the side. The woman is originally from Ukraine, and she is very stylish. I love her looks!

What's your favourite spot in the city to relax or recharge?

Well, for me, I don't need too much quiet… I like constant action and people around me. But Miradouro da Graça is always beautiful. For sitting outside, the river promenade Ribeira das Naus. Also fun is *Sunset Destination*, a hostel inside Cais do Sodré station—it has a rooftop terrace with a great view of the river. For recharging, I really like to dance. When I'm stressed,

LuxFrágil
Alfama

Damas
Graça

Bar 49
Bairro Alto

Tartine
Baixa

Piriquita II
Sintra

Planeta Bio
Príncipe Real

Jardim dos Sentidos
Príncipe Real

Arco-Íris
Santo António

A Ginjinha
Baixa

Casa Independente
Mouraria

Fábrica dos Sabores
Arroios

Espaço B
Príncipe Real

**Deposito da
Marinha Grande**
Estrela

Pap'Arcorda
São Paulo

Jardim de Estrela
Estrela

Café Tati
São Paulo

I go to *LuxFrágil* and dance it away! Or to *Damas* or *Bar 49*. Teatro do Bairro is also quite cool.

What about a nice coffee?

Tartine in Lisbon is a great, cool coffee shop with its own bakery. Outside Lisbon in Sintra, there's a great café called *Piriquita II*. I love to go there in December when the whole of Sintra is full of Christmas lights, to drink hot chocolate and eat the local cake "travesseiro" (puff pastry with almond cream).

Imagine I'm coming for the weekend, where would we go? Say Friday night to eat?

I'd choose a vegetarian option—there are two near Avenida Liberdade: *Planeta Bio* and *Jardim dos Sentidos*. Though perhaps better for lunch. There's another nearby called *Arco-Íris*, which is vegetarian and macrobiotic. After dinner we'd pass by *A Ginjinha*, a small bar where they sell the traditional Portuguese liquor of the same name, made from cherries and aguardente. Then we'd go to *Damas* or *Casa Independente*. We'd stay till 3 or 4am, and then off to *LuxFrágil!* I love to stay at Lux until the sun comes up, staying on the balconies overlooking the river, watching the sunrise with the night crowd. Oh, and at Lux, you should try the Luxini drinks—made with Lisbon's famous Santini ice cream.

And where would we go the next day?

Not too early—we'd take you for brunch. There are many places in our neighbourhood. One is *Fábrica dos Sabores*. After brunch, we'd shop around Príncipe Real. There are several nice shops, but I recommend *Espaço B* for clothes and design. And there's a small kiosk in the middle of the square to have coffee. If you're looking for a souvenir—at *Deposito da Marinha Grande* you can find glass objects and ceramics for a good price. For dinner I'd invite friends to my place and cook—it's what I normally do, instead of going to a restaurant.

So, would you cook traditional Portuguese dishes?

I can't cook them like my grandmother, who's an amazing cook—like many grandmothers in Portugal. But I love the traditional dishes: "favas" (green beans with chorizo sausage), "carapaus fritos" (fried mackerel) or "farinheira". The last is a chicken sausage invented by Jews in Portugal so they could pretend they were eating pork and not be identified as Jewish.

Can you recommend restaurants for these traditional dishes?

Not a specific one, but many! Every neighbourhood has several "tascas" (taverns)—they all serve solid quality. Oh, my favourite Portuguese dish is "Acorda de Marisco", a recipe from Alentejo. It's a bread soup made with lots of the best olive oil and garlic. It used to be a poor person's dinner, but it's evolved with all kinds of ingredients. My favourite is with prawns. It's best at *Pap'Arcorda* restaurant, near Cais do Sodré.

Back to the perfect weekend—where to listen to music?

There is this series of outdoor concerts called "Out Jazz" on summer weekends that started in *Jardim de Estrela*—which is a very nice park anyway. People sit in the grass and picnic while listening to various concerts. Another place I like to go for concerts—fado and jazz—is *Café Tati*. It's more relaxed than traditional fado bars, where the audience and the musician disapprove of any conversation during the performances.

Café Tati is the place to listen to the mournful melodies of Portuguese fado music without getting too formal

MUDE Museu do
Design e da Moda
Baixa

Restaurante
Ponto Final
Cacilhas

What about to take in some art?
The different museums in the Gulbenkian Park offer a distinctive selection of artists—there's always something to discover. And of course, I like *MUDE* (Museu do design e da moda), with exhibitions on fashion and product design.

And a day at the beach?
My favourite is Praia das Avencas. You can go by train, which is great, because most beaches around Lisbon can only be reached by car. Get off at Parede station, walk a few minutes and you're there. There are more small beaches like that along the railway from Lisbon's Cais do Sodré station to Cascais, and the ride itself is picturesque as it follows the coastline. If you're going by car though, go to Caparica, which has several beaches and quiet dunes—my favourite beach there is Praia da Rainha. Along the beach you'll find several small restaurants and bars, but there are also very quiet parts.

Where could we get the best seafood?
A great and affordable place is the small town of Cacilhas. It's on the other side of the river—ten minutes by ferry from Cais do Sodré. Cacilhas has several marisquerias (seafood places) and the walk to the end of the pier leads to *Restaurante Ponto Final*—a charming restaurant with a full view of Lisbon. That's also one of my favourite places!

And finally, anywhere in Lisbon you haven't been to, but would like to?
The EKA Palace gallery—for one of the legendary afterparties held there. The party crowd who finish at LuxFrágil at sunrise meet there on Saturday mornings. I'll definitely go this summer!

Entre Nós

A showcase by
Pauliana Valente Pimentel

Parallel universes are presented by the prominent Lisbon-born photographer, namely a forgotten area in Paris (Goutte d'Or) and one in Lisbon (Rua do Benformoso). The original installation also involved video artist Hélène Veiga Gomes. Pauliana's exhibition "Quel Pedra", shot in Cape Verde, has been supported by the prestigious Novo Banco prize and Lisbon's Museu Colecção Berardo

Kalaf Epalanga
As frontman for renowned kuduro band Buraka Som Sistema, he brought a bit of his native Angola to every corner of the world. These days his main focus is writing, design and finding a way to bring his global musical collective together

Kalaf Epalanga, Musician/Poet

Lyrical and Local

Kalaf Epalanga is a modern renaissance man, making his experience of Lisbon—where he relocated over two decades ago—a truly comprehensive one. Here, the poet and musician takes us for a night out and a memorable tram ride through town

Park
Estrela

B.Leza
São Paulo

Docks
São Paulo

LuxFrágil
Alfama

What's your relationship with Lisbon?

It's funny, people ask me "was it difficult to adapt?" But I come from a really urban society. Luanda is as busy and chaotic as any other Western city. Lisbon is kind of like an extension of our capital. I've bumped into my schoolmates from high school in the city. The wave of immigration that began in the 1970s settled down mostly in Lisbon, so it's easy to find Angolan restaurants and hairdressers. I can't really say a number because Portugal doesn't have statistics on the amount of Africans in the country, but roughly, Angolans make up the second-largest part of the African community in Lisbon, which is something in the hundreds of thousands of people. There are certain parts of the city that are almost like an African city. In fact, the name of our band came from one of those neighbourhoods, Buraka. We wanted to pay homage to the fact that those places are really diverse and multicultural.

And what about Buraka Som Sistema? You're finishing up your last tour—what now?

We're like a big family. We still have the label and we're like a collective—that's kind of our approach to music now. We just had the last Buraka tour and we're going to go on hiatus but we'll still be doing music and we still want to create. We want to turn Lisbon into this global club music capital. We've been doing a lot of work with people from Peru, Mexico, Angola. Once a year we want to gather with all these people and celebrate the music we cherish. So that's the plan after retirement, to dedicate more energy into turning this project into something more.

You've said you discovered electronic music after moving to Europe. What's

the Lisbon dance music scene like?

The music scene here is very eclectic. From hip-hop to drum 'n' bass, we have almost all the music genres represented in the city. Plus, the music scene is going through one of its most interesting periods in recent memory. The amount of kids making and playing all sorts of electronic music is at an all-time high, with plenty of good artists coming up with their own particular styles. With Lisbon in the middle of this musical Bermuda Triangle, which connects Africa with South America and the United Kingdom, there is fertile ground for a very hybrid and diverse musical output, with styles like zouk bass, afro-house or kuduro becoming bigger every year. There are the more traditional house and techno clubs, which are still the majority and range from the super cheesy to the very cool, and there's also a whole scene of African clubs, where one goes to dance kizomba and other styles of popular African music. There aren't that many big venues in general, but most of the time you get the feeling that there's a little bit of everything going on. Most clubs go on until the sun rises, giving way to the after-hours clubs, which then give way to the matinées, allowing you to party for a straight weekend if you're up for it.

And what would that party look like for us?

It would start out at a bar above a car park called *Park*. Then we'd go down the hill to the African clubs by the river, one is a Cape Verdean club called *B.Leza*, and there's another typical Angolan club night at *Docks*. This would be around 1 or 2am. Around 4 we'd go to another riverfront club called *LuxFrágil*. We have a residency and throw a party there every two

Billionaire José Berardo's staggering collection of modern Western art is on display at the Museu Colecção Berardo

Associação
Caboverdeana
Santo António

Cantinho do Aziz
Mouraria

months. If am still involved with club culture when I grow old, I want to be like the guy who owns that club. He's the godfather of the Lisbon club scene, Manuel Reis. He's the most advanced guy when it comes to music; he's very open. In that club you have hip hop nights, kuduro nights, you have the global dance music that we bring in, straight-up techno, house. It's all present in their programming and it really reflects what the Lisbon night is like.

Eating foreign cuisine can be a cultural exploration: where can we get a real taste of Angola in Lisbon?
The thing that made me fall in love with Lisbon was the fact that I could experience other Portuguese-speaking countries in one place. So you can go and have an amazing Brazilian night out or you can go and enjoy Mozambican food, which is something you can't find in very many places. I'd recommend three different African restaurants: One is the *Associação Caboverdeana*. It's in the middle of a business quarter so you have all the bankers and insurance brokers there, and in the middle of the day they take their ties and jackets off and dance to live music. On Tuesdays and Thursdays they serve some of the best "cachupa", a Cape Verdean bean, meat and corn stew that has to be cooked slowly. Then there's *Cantinho do Aziz*, a family-run restaurant founded by Aziz, a Mozambican man who moved to Lisbon in the 1980s and opened this monument to African gastronomy. I love the Zambezian chicken, but the shrimp and crab makoufe and the lamb chacuti also attract legions of loyal customers.

Poema do Semba
São Paulo

Feira da Ladra
Alfama

Discolecção
Bairro Alto

Lidija Kolovrat
Príncipe Real

Alexandra Moura
Príncipe Real

Underdogs
Beato

Montana
São Paulo

Livraria Histórica
e Ultramarina
Estrela

Livraria Antiquária
do Calhariz
Bairro Alto

Finally, one of those responsible for spreading the influence of kizomba and semba in Portugal is Paulo Flores, one of our most influential Angolan artists. In 2015 he opened *Poema do Semba* and it immediately became our unofficial cultural centre.

Any good places to go shopping for records?

You can combine some touristy activity with record-digging by going to a flea market called *Feira da Ladra*. Lisbon is full of hills and it's on one of the most famous hills, Graça. All the record dealers have their stands and you can find some gems. And there's also *Discolecção*. They have everything from psychedelic rock to African music, and you can find some great Brazilian stuff.

You've also been involved in fashion. How did that come about?

My relationship with design came about organically. I love the architecture of things, which is why I wear suits. But I also love the architecture of a t-shirt, the most amazing piece of clothing ever made. It's so simple, so democratic. I love democratic things. Of course you can wear a 1,000 euro t-shirt —which is stupid—but if you put a person wearing a 1,000 euro t-shirt and one wearing a 5 euro t-shirt side by side, you might not be able to spot the difference. That's what I love about design, it can be really democratic. I really believe design can make things better. Not just the practical aspect of it, but also in the emotional sense.

Any favourite places to pick up good Lisbon design?

The street to visit is Don Pedro V. It has become a place for fashion and design in recent years. Two of my favourite designers, *Lidija Kolovrat* and *Alexandra Moura*, have their shops and studios there.

Going back to democratic art— where can we find art on the streets of Lisbon?

There are several aspects that make Lisbon a unique place for street art. Some believe the 1974 revolution inspired people to take a stand and claim the streets, using the walls to express their thoughts and aspirations. Lisbon created Vhils, the city's main guy for street art. He directed one of our videos, and he has a gallery called *Underdogs* that is very active on the street art scene. They fly over a lot of big artists to paint murals. And then there's also the *Montana* shop. But the best place to see street art is actually in the streets. Lisbon is very proud of its scene, and you can spot some street art at Avenida Fontes Pereira de Melo where SAM3 and Os Gémeos painted the façade of two huge abandoned buildings. The Lisbon city council supports the Galeria Arte Urbana project and every two months they have new graffiti artists painting at Calçada da Glória near the beautiful Jardim São Pedro de Alcântara.

Aside from music and design, writing is another passion of yours. Is there good book shopping in Lisbon?

Lisbon is quite an old city, so you have what we call "Alfarrabistas" all over the city where you can find second-hand books, like the *Livraria Histórica e Ultramarina* and the *Livraria Antiquária do Calhariz*. Entering those places is like visiting a museum, and you can find some rare things like old editions of work by Fernando Pessoa, one of the writers who defined Portuguese literature. Lisbon is a city that really nurtured and gave birth to a lot of poets, it has a strong relationship with literature. We used to have an African bookshop that closed down, which is a pity.

Working with street artists from around the world, Underdogs gallery has a packed artistic programme and a great café

Cemitério dos
Prazeres
Campo do Ourique

MAAT Museum
Estrela

Centro Cultural
de Belém
Belém

Museu Colecção
Berardo
Belém

What in your opinion would be the best way to get lost in Lisbon? Take us on a journey through the city at its best.

The best is to buy a day ticket for transport. Two metro lines great for this are the 28 and the 15. Lisbon is the city of seven hills and the 28 crosses almost all of them. You can visit the flea market and do some record digging, go to Chiado and visit the Alfarrabistas, then see our parliament, which we're very proud of. When you get to the last hill, Campo do Ourique, there's a beautiful cemetery called *Cemitério dos Prazeres*. Some of the most prominent cultural figures of our country are resting there. And the 15 goes from Baixa all along the river. The view is amazing. It ends at Belém, which is where the ships sailed from to discover the world. In Belém you'll find three important museums, including the new *MAAT museum*, the *Centro Cultural de Belém* and the *Museu Colecção Berardo*, which is free.

Under the Radar

Just south of Lisbon's trendy Príncipe Real, the area around Praça das Flores and São Bento street is its shy little sister—neglected only by those unaware of its virtues. Here are some pointers to remedy that, from authentic cuisine to ice cream, markets and antique troves

| Shop | Take it Home |

Resist buying on beautiful, tourist-trap streets like Rua Augusta. Around São Bento the Portuguese products are better in quality and value. *Carinho do Vinho*'s owner is a lover of Portuguese wine who'll let you try before you buy. A few metres away, *Loja das Conservas* works as a node for the canned fish industry. Don't miss the mackerel fillet with spicy pickles and sardine eggs in olive oil. *Denegro* is where pastry chef António Marques creates chocolate bars, port truffles and smoky bonbons with Callebaut chocolate. *O Cocho* is a grocery shop dedicated to the southern region of Alentejo. Its shelves are filled with wine, olive oil, bread, cheese and sweets made with plenty of sugar and egg yolk. And for a less perishable investment, fashion boutique *+351*—named after the country's dialling code—deals in creations by Ana Penha e Costa. A former Billabong designer, she now develops women's and men's collections, accessories and beachwear.

● Estrela, various locations, see Index p. 64

Plenty of Fish

Portugal is a pescatarian paradise but the custom of buying from local markets has waned. *Peixaria Centenária* hopes to change that by funking up your fish purchase. The shop was created by a designer whose family have a long fishing history—the locally sourced fish are all reeled in by his grandfather. The surprising transformation in an old-school business comes from using non-smelly, leakproof bags, stylish illustrations of the products, orders of the day on the walls, and a sharp Instagram account.
• Peixaria Centenária, Praça das Flores, 55, Estrela, peixariacentenaria.pt

Culture   Art Crawl

To nibble on local culture instead, the area has options for diverse palates. Tucked down an anonymous alleyway, the *Atelier-Museu Júlio Pomar* explores the work of one of the country's most important artists. Pomar has worked over seven decades through many different phases. As a "neorealist" painter he was a vocal opponent of the Salazar regime in the 1940s. Meanwhile, *Casa dos Mundos* provides a canvas for social projects and exhibitions, and a venue for arts, music and dance festival "Todos" every September. Finally, a visit to *Zaratan* gallery might yield a vernissage, concert or book release.
• Estrela, various locations, see Index p. 64

Food   Cream Dream

When someone named Constanza Ventura is making the ice cream, you know you're getting real gelato italiano. Her *Gelateria Nannarella* is a popular ice cream shop just across the road from the little São Bento market. The place only fits two at once, so be prepared to wait in line for your afternoon sugar rush. On a hot day it can stretch around the corner, but it's worth it. Go for the "fior di panna" flavour and top with some homemade cream. Dreamy.
• Gelateria Nannarella, R. Nova da Piedade, 68, Estrela

Eat Well, Wait Less

Instead of waiting hours to eat in the over-hyped places of Príncipe Real, Praça das Flores offers an easier ride into local cuisine. Owned by veteran chef Miguel Castro e Silva, *De Castro* (Príncipe Real) seduces with its garden-facing terrace and interpretation of Portuguese dishes. Try the fried cod, "pica-pau"—a dish with chopped sausage in sauce—and veal pastries. The cream-topped Marrare steak has been a specialty at *Café de São Bento* (Estrela) for 30 years—ring the bell to get in. And *Dona Quitéria* (Príncipe Real) occupies a 19th-century grocery. Taste the monkfish rice while admiring old bottles and porcelain dogs.
• Various locations, see Index p. 64

Food   Sweet Thing

On a shy corner of Praça das Flores, *O Bolo da Nonna* is a tiny place where the tables are made of sewing machines and the ceilings covered in frescos. The core of the business is explicit as soon as you cross the front door: a showcase full of cakes forces you to consider dessert, even at 10am. When in doubt—they serve orange and meringue cake or salted caramel pancakes—go for the chocolate cake, whose beloved recipe was reason enough for the owner to open this spot.
• O Bolo da Nonna, Praça das Flores 41, Estrela

Night   Old School Tipples

On one hand you have an art deco bar, *Foxtrot*, where the waiter brings your tobacco to the table, you can play snooker and smoke while drinking an Old Fashioned, you have to ring the bell to enter and you can ask a valet to park your car. A short walk away, you won't lack for topics of conversation at the *Pavilhão Chines* (Príncipe Real). Its five rooms are packed with fascinating bric-à-brac collected over 70 years by the late owner. Pool tables provide yet another distraction. Order a drink from the smart barmen (pictured) and absorb the atmosphere.
• Various locations, see Index p. 64

Shop | **Olden Goldies**

For some people, "São Bento" is a name asssociated with the Portuguese parliament—where the country's bigwigs play their power games and demonstrators gather by the grand staircase. For others, it signifies the long street of Rua de São Bento—where more than 20 antique and vintage stores offer the potential deal of a lifetime. Besides the classic antique dealers like *O Marquês* or *Miguel Arruda*, find Scandinavian furniture at *América Móvel* or 1960s lamps and neon signs at *MacWall & Floor*. A standout is *Cavalo de Pau* (pictured), with its careful curation of antique, vintage and contemporary pieces. You might not want to ship chairs and tables home, but rugs, wooden masks and other pieces are more transportable. The "rocking horse" has been a mainstay on antique street for around two decades. Even older, at more than 90 years of age, is *O Barateiro da Casa Amarela*. You can spot it easily from its bright yellow façade with chamber-pots cheerfully hanging at the entrance. Pass the threshold to a space of old-world charm, with old pots, radios and TVs stacked up its walls.

• Estrela, various locations, see Index p. 64

Thiago Pais, Food Writer
Mixed Grill

<u>Thiago Pais</u>
He certainly worked hard to avoid his calling. Lisbon native Thiago Pais tried out many things: advertising, sports and music journalism, PR work—and even worked for NATO in Brussels. But in the end his passion prevailed and he became a food writer. His book "As 50 Melhores Tascas de Lisboa" is a perfect accompaniment to a trip round Lisbon's taverns

From being spoon-fed by a premium chef and enjoying fatty sardines from the grill, to African and Brazilian excellence and a two-starred fusion standout... It isn't easy deciding where to eat in Lisbon, unless you ask an expert. Thiago Pais helps us sort the options

Merendinha do Arco
Baixa

Cartaxinho
Santo António

Faz Frio
Príncipe Real

Manteigaria
Bairro Alto

Cervejaria Ramiro
Intendente

Nune's Marisqueira
Belém

Cervejaria O
Pinóquio
Bairro Alto

Ibo Marisqueira
São Paulo

Mar do Inferno
Cascais

Restaurante Adraga
Colares

Adega da Bairrada
Alvalade

Imperial de Campo
de Ourique
Campo de Ourique

Maçã Verde
Alfama

What are authentic signature dishes from the Lisbon region?

There's something curious about that: there aren't many signature dishes originally from Lisbon. Actually, it is also very difficult to find someone whose family is originally from Lisbon, because it is always been a city of comers and goers, with very mixed influences. Of course there are some dishes the city adopted or were created in small restaurants like "bacalhau à Brás" (cod with egg and fried potatoes), "peixinhos da horta", a kind of vegetable tempura, "pataniscas de bacalhau" (cod tempura) or even some sweet stuff like the very famous "pastéis de nata" (custard tart).

Where can we get them?

Fortunately you can find them almost everywhere. There are maybe hundreds of small, humble, family-owned, traditional restaurants all over the city that serve these kind of dishes. You don't have to look that hard. But for pataniscas I'd recommend *Merendinha do Arco*. For bacalhau à Brás I'd say *O Cartaxinho*—they serve it on Mondays, or *Faz Frio* where it's the dish of the day every Friday. For pastéis de nata I wouldn't think twice: *Manteigaria*. They're even better, in my opinion, than at the famous Fábrica dos Pastéis de Belém.

The Atlantic Ocean is right in front of your door… Where and what is the freshest seafood?

Once again, it's not hard to find restaurant storefronts filled with seafood and fish. But for this kind of stuff you should really know where to go. Not only because some seafood might be a bit expensive, but also because only the most popular restaurants have enough product rotation to ensure complete freshness in everything they serve.

Cervejaria Ramiro is an obvious choice—as the daily queues indicate. But alternatives include *Nune's Marisqueira*, *Pinóquio*, or *Ibo Marisqueira*. If you want to make a short trip to Cascais and the beaches around there you can also find excellent seafood, namely at *Mar do Inferno* or *Adraga*.

What is a local fish you would recommend?

During the summer, sardines are a big thing here. Every restaurant or house with a grill will use it for sardines at some point. But usually, they are only good—fat and juicy, I mean—from July on. Lately, there's been an effort by some people to diversify the kind of fish we consume here: for example, the formerly disregarded mackerel is now being used by lots of chefs, even in fine dining.

You've written a book about the 50 best "tascas". Can you explain what those are?

A tasca is what we call a cheap, traditional, honest restaurant, where you can eat and drink a lot and pay less than 10 euros. Or maybe 15 if you go for a bottle of wine instead of beer. There's a set of traditional Portuguese dishes almost all of them serve, like "cozido à portuguesa" (stew with different meats and vegetables), "feijoada" (bean stew) or a variety of grilled meat and fish. Nevertheless, some tascas specialise in a dish or two, which are usually served on a specific day of the week.

Which ones are not to miss?

In my book, I highlighted seven tascas, for which I created the Golden Toothpick Award ("Palito d'Ouro". I'd say these give you a pretty good summary. They are: *Adega da Bairrada*, *Imperial de Campo de Ourique*, *Maçã Verde*,

Stop do Bairro
Campo de Ourique

Zé Pinto
Benfica

Zapata
Estrela

Zé da Mouraria
Mouraria

Boi-Cavalo
Alfama

Leopold
Mouraria

Restaurante Apicius
Estrela

Belcanto
Baixa

Loco
Estrela

Cantinho da Paz
Estrela

Jesus é Goês
Santo António

Aromas & Temperos
Arroios

Casa Mocambo
Graça

Afro Tas'ka
Bairro Alto

Café do Paço
Intendente

Pizzeria Casanova
Alfama

Park
Estrela

Stop do Bairro, Zé Pinto, Zapata and *Zé da Mouraria.*

Who are the key chefs for Portuguese food with a creative spin?

There are a few chefs bringing new ideas, each one in his own way and not necessarily in classic "fine dining" restaurants. For instance, Hugo Brito from *Boi-Cavalo*, Tiago Feio from *Leopold* or the couple Francisco Magalhães and Joana Xardoné from *Apicius*. In the fine dining scene I'd have to mention, obviously, José Avillez from *Belcanto*, the only two-Michelin-starred restaurant in Lisbon, but also Henrique Sá Pessoa, João Rodrigues, Ljubomir Stanisic, Alexandre Silva, Vítor Claro... The list could go on and on. Fortunately, we're going through a very fertile moment in cuisine creativity here.

And who is the most forward-thinking chef in Portugal for you?

I had a stunning experience at Alexandre Silva's *Loco*. It's unique from the moment you sit down to the moment you walk out. The bread is hanging over your head, the snacks are served fast—some are even served to the client's mouth by the chef himself. And his dishes completely reinvent some very well known Portuguese flavors. On top of that, they brew their own beer and ferment juices. I know all of that has been done in some places around the world before, but never like that, and never in Lisbon.

You have also lots of kitchens from the former colonies: e.g. Brazilian, African. Any tips?

We have some excellent Goese—from Goa, in India—restaurants, like *Cantinho da Paz* or *Jesus é Goês*. But you have to like spicy food to go there. Recently, a young Brazilian chef opened a very small restaurant, *Aromas & Temperos*, that mixes

Portuguese and Brazilian flavours and ingredients quite well. And the African scene is dynamic—I know of two restaurants that have opened in the last month. I've been hearing good things about both of them: *Casa Mocambo* and *Afro Tas'ka.*

What is your personal favourite restaurant in town and why?

I go to too many restaurants on a weekly basis to have a favourite one. Having said that, there are places where I feel right at home like *Café do Paço*, *Pizzeria Casanova* and the aforementioned Zé da Mouraria and Stop do Bairro.

And after dinner—where do you enjoy a drink or two?

If it's hot out there, preferably in a place with a terrace like *Park* or *Topo*—both with rooftops. If I want a fancy cocktail, which doesn't happen frequently, I'll choose something like *Cinco Lounge* or *Red Frog*, a fairly new speakeasy bar.

Where would you go for a romantic trip out of town with your lady—and where would you have dinner?

Somewhere in the southwest coast of the country, from Tróia to Odeceixe. That's still the best area to run away from the city's madness. Hopefully, we'd end up at *Azenha do Mar*, between Zambujeira and Odeceixe, where I know she loves the "feijoada de búzios" (bean stew with whelks) and I love the "arroz de marisco" (seafood rice).

What local cheeses and cold meats should we know about? And where to buy them for a nice picnic?

If you're a fan of cheese you'll be happy once you get here. Portugal has some of the best cheeses in the world, either soft, like the famous Queijo da Serra or hard, like the Sao Jorge, named after the Azorean island it comes from. My favourite

José Avillez's Belcanto took just two years to win two Michelin stars for its twist on Portuguese cuisine in a ten-table setting

Topo
Mouraria

Cinco Lounge
Príncipe Real

Red Frog Speakeasy
Príncipe Real

Azenha do Mar
Odemira

Manteigaria Silva
Baixa

place to buy these kind of products is *Manteigaria Silva*, next to Rossio. Not only because of its great variety but also because the salespeople know everything there is to know about cheese and cold meats. And they'll teach you. Speaking of cold meats: try every kind of ham, blood sausage and chorizo from the Alentejo region, especially those made with the Iberian black pork meat. After you fill your picnic basket go to a place near the river, like Ribeira das Naus. You can't ask for a better view.

Apart from endless feasting—what else is not to be missed in Lisbon?
  A Benfica game—but I'm biased—and the river. Just walking along it can make you feel years younger. And it can also help burn some calories from all the eating and drinking.

Gisela João, Singer

Frontier of Fado

Gisela João
She is hailed as a symbol of the new generation of fado. Born in Barcelos, she moved to Lisbon in 2009. There, she began to sing at Sr. Vinho, fado house of acclaimed singer Maria da Fé. A hit concert at nightclub LuxFrágil led up to her 2013 debut album, "Gisela João"—chosen as Portuguese album of the year. She now divides time between Lisbon and touring the world

Lisbon blends antique and modern, and Gisela embraces the two. Though she's partial to a night clubbing to dance music, she's most inspired by the traditional scene: from the historic districts where people still speak to neighbours from their windows, to the vantage points, where you can embrace the city with your eyes

Zapata
Estrela

Tasca Bela
Alfama

Maria da Mouraria
Mouraria

Sr. Vinho
Estrela

Discoteca Amália
Baixa

What most surprised you about Lisbon when you came to live here?

The light. I think everyone says this, but it's true. Despite all the bitterness of life, the city breathes life into those who live here thanks to its light. Let's assume that a year has 1,600 days: the chances of waking up 1,450 days a year with a smile on my face because of the sun that enters through my window is very high.

You've always chosen to live in historic areas like Mouraria and Prazeres. Why?

These are neighbourhoods that are in the centre of the big city, but feel like villages. People know each other, talk with neighbours, women hang their clothes and chat by the windows, old ladies knit on the street, people go in their bathrobes to buy bread. I have travelled a lot but never seen this happen in any other big city. I love this. To be able to see this real life, to be able to walk in the city centre from one end to the other in a short time, and to feel safe while doing so; Lisbon still has all of this.

When you return from touring to Lisbon, what's the first thing you feel like doing?

Going to eat a "bitoque". Why is it so hard to find a good grilled steak with chips, salad, and fried egg outside of Portugal? I don't understand it. I often go to *Zapata* on Poço dos Negros street, which is super Portuguese, with homemade food. The owners are from Minho— it seems they're always grumbling but it's just the typical humour from the north. After that I usually go for a walk through Chiado, if possible. I go to Calçada do Combro, which is beautiful, down to Rossio, and onwards to Ribeira das Naus to see the river. I sit there a while, it knows me so well. It seems like a

cliché to do this route, but it's like seeing the city for the first time. I feel at home.

When you fancy listening to fado and having a drink with friends, where do you go?

There are two places: *Tasca Bela*, in Alfama, and *Maria da Mouraria*, managed by the fado singer Hélder Moutinho. In both of these places, it's easy to feel at home. They have good snacks, a relaxed atmosphere, and although they're not fado houses, they always have a resident artist who sings well. From time to time I also go to *Sr. Vinho* when I have a longing for it, but it's kind of a more formal atmosphere. For me, they have the best guitar duo of all the Lisbon fado houses. And a range of extremely high-level singers.

If someone who's never experienced fado asks for a recommendation, what would you suggest?

Nowadays it's very easy to be fooled. Many fado houses are designed for tourists, and the experience turns out to be less than ideal. Suggesting a place depends on the type of person you are—if you like formal settings or not, and your budget. Expensive does not necessarily mean good. But just having fun is also no good. I don't want people at fado for the first time to leave thinking it is just funny, like a cook coming out of the kitchen with a shawl on her back, singing a few things. Fado is supposed to make you feel some-thing inside, to take your breath away. Perhaps the three examples I gave above are the ones I'd recommend—in general, they are good experiences.

And where can fado CDs be found?

On Rua do Ouro, the store *Discoteca Amália* has plenty. On

Carrinha do Fado
Baixa

Feira da Ladra
Alfama

Retrosaria
Bairro Alto

A Vida Portuguesa
Intendente

LuxFrágil
Alfama

Bar Oslo
São Paulo

Music Box
São Paulo

MM Café
Areeiro

Tasca Nelo
Príncipe Real

Cacau da Ribeira
São Paulo

Rua do Carmo, there's also a mobile store, the *Carrinha do Fado* (fado wagon), which is very cute, and the owner is super friendly. But if you want to find older records in vinyl, or the works of less famous singers who tell the story of fado—not just Amália Rodrigues—there's nothing like the *Feira da Ladra* (flea market), on Tuesdays and Saturdays. It has everything, and is a great day out.

Your followers know you're a fan of traditional crafts such as embroidery from Minho. Where to buy traditional products beyond the souvenir shops?

There is a shop on Rua do Loreto called *Retrosaria*, by Rosa Pomar. It's hidden on the second floor and has very original pieces. They also hold workshops on Portuguese wool, knitting, and embroidery. Those who have time should enroll in one of the workshops; these crafts are part of our tradition. It is also impossible not to mention the store *A Vida Portuguesa*. They have everything you can imagine there, it is indispensable.

You've been known to shake up the traditions. You took fado into clubs, you wear trainers, you admit to liking electronic music, and you invite your audience to go dancing after the show. Where do you go dancing in Lisbon?

LuxFrágil is a hot spot. It's guaranteed to always have good music, and is a great point of reference in the city. But to start the night when I'm with friends, I really like *Oslo* at Cais do Sodré. It's so bad it's good. It has that environment that's very "basfond", like an old brothel, and full of mirrors—it feels like you're in a movie. They always play hits from the 1980s and 1990s that everyone knows and can dance to non-stop. It doesn't matter if it's David Bowie or Bananarama.

Then I like to go to *Music Box* for a dance before going to Lux. Evenings always end there. On weekdays, *MM Café* at the Teatro Maria Matos is a good option. It has a more alternative events programme, which appeals to me.

At the end of a long night, are there still spots open for early-hours eating?

Of course there are! The *Nelo* "tasca" (tavern) on Rua do Telhal is a classic among fado artists. It opens just after midnight and goes on until morning, it is the meeting point for many people seeking a late-night snack. Then there's always *Cacau da Ribeira*. I'm nocturnal, but I don't like to get home in the morning. For me, it's the stories of the day that fuel the fado.

If you had to leave Lisbon forever, where would you take a last look at the city?

At the vantage point of Senhora do Monte. It has just a small church next door and no kiosks, making it more quiet and untouched than others. Then there's that view that stretches to the River Tagus, it seems to embrace Lisbon, as if you are in the movie "Titanic". It's probably one of the most beautiful sunsets in the city.

Named after fado queen Amália Rodrigues, this store's records are bound to induce some serious saudade

Frontier of Fado

Bugigangas

Put a Cork On It

Pelcor's cork umbrella makes great use of Portugal's biggest export material without screaming "souvenir". Sustainable harvesting means the cork oak trees age for 25 years before the nine-year harvest cycles begin. How's that for singing in the rain?
• Cork Tall Umbrella, Pelcor, Pátio do Tijolo, Loja 4, pelcor.pt

Sweet Nostalgia

Forget Mast Brothers—Regina was making chocolate cool in the 1960s. Founded in 1928 in Lisbon, the candy company later decided to cater to tourists with beautiful postcard-like packaging. The designs have now been revived to the delight of visiting retrophiles.
• Chocolates Regina, chocolatesregina.com

Ray of Light

People can't stop talking about Lisbon's light. Bring some home, courtesy of design studio Branca Lisboa's sleek "Raio T" tabletop lamp. The collection will have you seriously considering those excess baggage fees.
• Raio T lamp, Branca Lisboa, Rua da Rosa, 40, branca-lisboa.com

Books

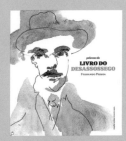

The Book of Disquiet
• Fernando Pessoa, 1982

They say Portugal's greatest four poets are Fernando Pessoa. That's because he wrote under various "heteronyms"—fully fledged personalities with differing histories and views. Compiled posthumously 50 years after Pessoa's death, this is a masterpiece of existentialism. Get the Richard Zenith translation.

Pereira Maintains
• Antonio Tabucchi, 1994

A second-rate newspaper editor in 1938 Lisbon—and quintessential anti-hero—wrestles with his conscience as the Salazar dictatorship shows its true colours. Italian writer Tabucchi was an expert on Portuguese literature.

Blindness
• Jose Saramago, 1995

Perhaps the most universal of the Portuguese Nobel laureate's groundbreaking novels. The story of a city torn apart by an epidemic of blindness presents a shocking dissection of society.

Films

Mysteries of Lisbon
• Raúl Ruiz, 2010

Prolific Chilean filmmaker Raúl Ruiz's epic last work drifts through the world of the 19th-century nobility with a cast of fascinating characters and a dreamlike pace bordering on surreality.

Casa de Lava
• Pedro Costa, 1994

A young nurse in Lisbon agrees to accompany an injured migrant worker home to volcano-stricken Cape Verde. Costa's unflinching portrayals of Lisbon's slum reality combined with his docu-realist approach have seen him lavished with the praise of arthouse critics.

RECORDAÇÕES DA CASA AMARELA

Recollections of the Yellow House
• João César Monteiro, 1989

An obsessive intellectual living in a seedy Lisbon hostel—brilliantly played by the director—shambolically lurches towards the nuthouse. A tragicomic snapshot of rundown Lisbon.

Music

Taxi
• Taxi, 1981

The first LP of the Portuguese rock giants contains their inimitable blend of ska and new wave, and several of their biggest hits. The lyrics were composed in English but recorded in Portuguese on request of label Polygram.

Miss Perfumado
• Cesaria Évora, 1992

"The Barefoot Diva" was discovered singing in a sailor's tavern in Lisbon in the 1980s and went on to record this double goldselling album in Paris. This classic of Cape Verdean morna music includes the uplifting "Angola", and "Sodade", a tribute to that bittersweet feeling.

Chorinho Feliz
• Maria João e Mario Laginha, 2012

This husband and wife duo, two of Portugal's most creative musicians, have often trodden the experimental outskirts of jazz. But this album represents a break from the avant-garde—an easierlistening celebration of Portuguese culture with a nod to Brazil.

Districts

1. West
Belém, Benfica, Campo de Ourique, Estrela, Príncipe Real

2. Central
Baixa, Bairro Alto, São Paulo, Santo António

3. Downtown
Alfama, Intendente, Graça, Mouraria

4. Northeast
Alvalade, Areeiro, Arroios, Avenidas Novas, Beato

5. Other

Index

© Culture
Ⓕ Food
Ⓝ Night
Ⓞ Outdoors
Ⓢ Shop

Have all these locations at your fingertips with the LOST iN mobile app

1. West

351
R. de São Bento 18
+351 913 273 075
mais351.pt
→ p.50 Ⓢ

Alexandra Moura
Embaixada 2°, Praça do Príncipe Real 26
+351 21 314 2511
alexandramoura.com
→ p.21, 46 Ⓢ

América Móvel
R. de São Bento 428
+351 213 963 260
americamovel.pt
→ p.53 Ⓢ

Atelier-Museu Júlio Pomar
R. Vale 7
+351 21 817 2111
ateliermuseu
juliopomar.pt
→ p.51 ©

Bar Foxtrot
Travessa Santa Teresa 28
+351 21 395 2697
barfoxtrot.pt → p.52 Ⓝ

Botanical Garden
R. da Escola Politécnica 54
+351 21 392 1800
→ p.16 Ⓞ

Café De São Bento
R. de São Bento 212
+351 21 395 2911
cafesaobento.com
→ p.52 Ⓕ

Carinho do Vinho
R. Nova da Piedade 23
+351 21 827 1872
→ p.50 Ⓢ

Casa dos Mundos
R. Nova da Piedade 66
→ p.51 ©

Cemitério dos Prazeres
Praça São João Bosco
cm-lisboa.pt → p.49 Ⓞ

Centro Cultural de Belém
Praça do Império
+351 21 361 2400
ccb.pt → p.49 ©

Cantinho da Paz
R. Paz 4
+351 21 390 1963
→ p.56 Ⓕ

Cavalo de Pau
R. de São Bento 164
+351 21 396 6605
cavalodepau.pt
→ p.53 Ⓢ

De Castro
R. Marcos Portugal 1
+351 21 590 3077
→ p.52 Ⓕ

Denegro
R. de S. Bento, n°333
+351 21 099 8022
denegro.pt → p.50 Ⓢ

Depósito da Marinha Grande
R. São Bento 159
+351 21 395 5818
dmg.com.pt → p.32 Ⓢ

Discoteca Luanda
Travessa Teixeira Júnior 6 → p.8 Ⓝ

Dona Quiteria
Travessa São José 1
+351 21 395 1521
→ p.52 Ⓕ

Espaço B
R. da Escola Politécnica 94
+351 21 397 9605
→ p.32 Ⓢ

Espaço Espelho d'Água
Av. Brasília 210
+351 21 301 0510
espacoespelhodeagua.com → p.6 ©

Gelataria Nannarella
R. Nova da Piedade 68
+351 926 878 553
→ p.51 Ⓕ

Jardim da Estrela
Praça da Estrela
→ p.32 Ⓞ

Jardim dos Sentidos
R. da Mãe de Água 3
+351 21 342 3670
jardimdossentidos.com
→ p.30 Ⓕ

Lidija Kolovrat
R. Dom Pedro V 79
+351 21 387 4536
lidijakolovrat.org
→ p.48 Ⓢ

Livraria Histórica E Ultramarina
R. de São Bento 644
+351 21 346 8589
→ p.48 Ⓢ

Loco
R. Navegantes 53
+351 21 396 1851
→ p.56 Ⓕ

Loja das Conservas
1200 182, R. do Arsenal 130
+351 911 181 210
→ p.50 Ⓢ

Macwall & Floor
R. de São Bento 285
+351 21 390 3375
→ p.53 Ⓢ

Mercado de Campo de Ourique
106, R. Coelho da Rocha 104 → p.11 Ⓕ

Miguel Arruda Antiguidades
R. de São Bento 356
+351 21 396 1165
arruda.pt → p.53 Ⓢ

Møbler
R. Nova da Piedade 41
+351 911 005 860
moblerstore.com
→ p.14 Ⓢ

Muito Muito at Lx Factory
R. Rodrigues de Faria 103
muitomuito.pt
→ p.14 Ⓢ

Museu Coleção Berardo
Praça do Império
+351 21 361 2878
museuberardo.pt
→ p.16 ©

Nune's Marisqueira
R. Bartolomeu Dias 120
+351 21 301 9899
→ p.55 Ⓕ

O Barateiro da Casa Amarela
R. de São Bento 294
→ p.53 Ⓢ

O Bolo da Nonna
Praça das Flores 41
+351 21 395 1231
→ p.52 Ⓕ

O Cocho
R. de São Bento 239
+351 912 376 675
ococho.com
→ p.50 Ⓢ

Park
Travessa da Condessa
do Rio 7
→ p.14, 46, 56 Ⓝ

Pavilhão Chines
R. Dom Pedro V 89
→ p.52 Ⓝ

P. T. Marquês
R. São Bento 394
+351 21 397 3462
→ p.53 Ⓢ

Peixaria Centenária
Praça das Flores 55
peixariacentenaria.pt
→ p.51 Ⓢ

Planeta Bio
Praça da Alegria 40
+351 21 809 2063
→ p.32 Ⓕ

Red Frog Speakeasy
R. do Salitre 5A
→ p.56 Ⓝ

Restaurante Apicius
R. da Cruz dos
Poiais 89
+351 21 390 0652
apicius.pt → p.56 Ⓕ

**Restaurante Imperial
de Campo de Ourique**
R. Correia Teles 67
+351 21 388 6096
→ p.55 Ⓕ

Sr. Vinho
R. Meio à Lapa 18
+351 21 397 2681
srvinho.com → p.59 Ⓕ

Stop do Bairro
R. Tenente Ferreira
Durão 55
+351 21 388 8856
→ p.56 Ⓕ

Tasca Nelo
R. do Telhal 11
→ p.60 Ⓕ

Zapata
R. do Poço dos
Negros 47
+351 21 390 8942
→ p.56, 59 Ⓕ

Zaratan
R. de São Bento 432
+351 965 218 382
zaratan.pt → p.51 Ⓒ

Zé Pinto
Largo General Sousa
Brandão 2
+351 21 778 7783
→ p.56 Ⓕ

2. Central

Afro Tas'ka
R. Marechal
Saldanha 13
+351 21 808 6930
→ p.56 Ⓕ

A Ginjinha
Praça Dom Pedro IV 71
→ p.32 Ⓝ

A Merendinha do Arco
R. dos Sapateiros 230
+351 21 342 5135
→ p.55 Ⓕ

Arco-Íris
R. São José 95
+351 21 355 7928
→ p.32 Ⓕ

**Associação
Caboverdeana**
R. Duque de Palmela 2
acaboverdeana.org
→ p.47 Ⓕ

Bar 49
R. da Barroca 49
→ p.24, 32 Ⓝ

Bar Oslo
R. Nova do
Carvalho 17
→ p.60 Ⓝ

B.Leza
Cais Gás 1
+351 21 010 6837
→ p.8, 15, 46 Ⓝ

Cacau Da Ribeira
Av. 24 de Julho
+351 21 342 1869
→ p.60 Ⓕ

Café Tati
R. Ribeira Nova 36
+351 21 346 1279
cafetati.blogspot.de
→ p.32 Ⓕ Ⓝ

Carrinha do Fado
R. do Carmo 51
→ p.60 Ⓢ

Cartaxinho
R. de Santa Marta 20
+351 21 356 2971
→ p.55 Ⓕ

Casa da Índia
R. do Loreto
+351 21 342 3661
→ p.60 Ⓕ

Cervejaria O Pinóquio
Praça dos
Restauradores 79
+351 21 346 5106
restaurantepinoquio.pt
→ p.55 Ⓕ

ComCor
R. Alexandre
Herculano 11E
+351 213 304 024
→ p.23 Ⓢ

Discolecção
Calçada do Duque 53
+351 21 347 1486
→ p.48 Ⓢ

Discoteca Amália
R. Áurea 272
+351 21 342 0939
→ p.59 Ⓢ

Docks Club
R. Da Cintura Do Porto
De Lisboa Edif 226
→ p.46 Ⓝ

Ibo Marisqueira
R. Cintura do Porto 22
+351 929 308 068
→ p.55 Ⓕ

Jesus é Goês
R. São José 23
+351 21 154 5812
→ p.56 Ⓕ

**Livraria Antiquária
do Calhariz**
Lr. do Calhariz, 14
→ p.48 Ⓢ

Luvaria Ulisses
R. do Carmo 87
luvariaulisses.com
→ p.40 Ⓕ

**Manteigaria Fábrica
de Pastéis de Nata**
R. do Loreto 2
+351 21 347 1492
→ p.55 Ⓕ

Manteigaria Silva
R. Dom Antão De
Almada 1
+351 21 342 4905
→ p.57 Ⓢ

Montana Lisboa
R. da Cintura, Porto de
Armazém A 20
+351 912 993 675
→ p.48 Ⓢ

**Museu do Design
e da Moda (MUDE)**
R. Augusta 24
mude.pt → p.33 Ⓒ

MusicBox
R. Nova do
Carvalho 24
+351 21 347 3188
musicboxlisboa.com
→ p.15 Ⓝ

Pap'Açorda
Av. 24 de Julho 49
+351 21 346 4811
papacorda.com
→ p.32 Ⓕ

Poema do Semba
Av. Dom Carlos I 140
+351 910 829 586
→ p.48 Ⓕ

Primeiros Sintomas
R. Ribeira Nova 44
+351 21 096 4851
primeiros-sintomas.
com → p.16 Ⓒ

Purex
241, R. Salgadeiras 28
→ p.24 Ⓝ

Restaurante Belcanto
Lgo. de São Carlos 10
+351 21 342 0607
belcanto.pt → p.56 Ⓕ

Restaurante Faz Frio
R. do Loreto 2
+351 21 347 1492
→ p.55 Ⓕ

Retrosaria
R. do Loreto 61
+351 21 347 3090
→ p.60 Ⓢ

Rua das Gaivotas 6
R. das Gaivotas 6
R.dasgaivotas6.pt
→ p.16, 24 Ⓒ

Slou
R. Nova da
Trindade 22E
+351 21 347 1104
sloulisbon.com
→ p.23 Ⓢ

Sneak Peek
R. Ivens, 8
+351 21 342 0499
→ p.23 Ⓢ

**Sunset Destination
Hostel**
Praça do Duque
de Terceira → p.31 Ⓝ

**Taberna da Rua
das Flores**
R. das Flores 103
+351 21 347 9418
→ p.15 Ⓕ

Tartine
R. Serpa Pinto 15A
+351 21 342 9108
tartine.pt → p.32 Ⓕ

Tasca Kome
R. da Madalena 57
+351 21 134 0117
kome-lisboa.com
→ p.15 Ⓕ

Tokyo
R. Nova do Carvalho 12
tokyo.com.pt → p.16 Ⓝ

3. Down-town

A Vida Portuguesa
Largo do Intendente
Pina Manique 23
+351 211 974 512
avidaportuguesa.com
→ p.19, 60 Ⓢ

Bar Anos 60
Largo Terreirinho 21
→ p.21 Ⓝ

Boi-Cavalo Restaurante
R. do Vigário 70
+351 21 887 1653
boi-cavalo.pt → p.56 Ⓕ

Café da Garagem
Costa do Castelo 75
+351 21 885 4190
teatrodagaragem.com
→ p.19 Ⓕ

Café do Paço
Paço da Rainha 62
+351 21 888 0185
→ p.56 Ⓕ

Camilla Watson Studio
Largo dos Trigueiros 16A
camillawatsonphoto
graphy.net → p.20 Ⓒ

Cantinho do Aziz
R. de São Lourenço 5
+351 21 887 6472
→ p.47 Ⓕ

Casa dos Amigos do Minho
R. do Benformoso 244
→ p.18 Ⓕ

Casa Independente
Largo do Intendente
Pina Manique 45
casaindependente.com
→ p.15, 21, 32 Ⓝ Ⓒ

Casa Mocambo
R. do Vale de Santo
António, 122A
→ p.56 Ⓕ

Cervejaria Ramiro
Av. Almirante Reis 1
cervejariaramiro.pt
→ p.24, 55 Ⓕ

Chapitô
Costa do Castelo 1
+351 21 885 5550
chapito.org → p.16 Ⓒ

Cortiço & Netos
Calçada de Santo
André 66
+351 21 136 2376
corticoenetos.com
→ p.20 Ⓢ

Cozinha Popular da Mouraria
R. das Olarias 5
+351 926 520 568
→ p.20 Ⓢ

Damas Bar
R. da Voz do
Operário 60
+351 964 964 416
→ p.24, 32 Ⓒ

Dhaka
R. do Benformoso 222
+351 920 492 645
dhakarestaurante.com
→ p.18 Ⓕ

Feira da Ladra
Campo de Santa Clara
+351 21 817 0800
cm-lisboa.pt
→ p.14, 48, 60 Ⓢ

Feira das Almas
Regueirão Anjos 70
feiradasalmas.org
→ p.31 Ⓢ

Leopold
R. São Cristóvão 27
+351 21 886 1697
→ p.56 Ⓕ

LuxFrágil
Av. Infante D.
Henrique, Armazém A
luxfragil.com → p.15,
24, 31, 46, 60 Ⓝ

Maçã Verde
R. Caminhos de Ferro 82
→ p.56 Ⓕ

Maria da Mouraria
Largo Severa 2B
+351 21 886 0165
mariadamouraria.pt
→ p.59 Ⓕ

No. 43, 2nd floor
R. do Benformoso 43
→ p.18 Ⓕ

Pho Pu
R. do Benformoso 76
+351 21 130 7473
→ p.18 Ⓕ

Pizzeria Casanova
Av. Infante Dom
Henrique Loja 7
+351 21 887 7532
→ p.16 Ⓕ

Tasca Bela
R. dos Remédios 190
→ p.8, 59 Ⓕ

Topo
Commercial Center
Martim Moniz, Praça
Martim Moniz
+351 21 588 1322
→ p.56 Ⓝ

Zé da Mouraria
R. João do Outeiro 24
+351 21 886 5436
→ p.19, 56 Ⓕ

4. Northeast

Adega da Bairrada
R. Reinaldo Ferreira 14
+351 21 848 2774
→ p.55 Ⓕ

Aromas e Temperos
Travessa Rebelo da
Silva 2
+351 21 362 0119
→ p.56 Ⓕ

**Calouste Gulbenkian
Museum & Gardens**
Av. de Berna 45 A
+351 21 782 3000
gulbenkian.pt
→ p.10, 16, 31 Ⓒ Ⓞ

**CAM – Centro de
Arte Moderna**
R. Doutor Nicolau
Bettencourt
+351 21 782 3800
gulbenkian.pt
→ p.10 Ⓒ

Cantinho do Vintage
Av. Infante Dom
Henrique A
+351 929 164 323
→ p.14 Ⓢ

Culturgest
R. Arco do Cego 77
→ p.16 Ⓒ

Fábrica dos Sabores
Av. Defensores de
Chaves 55
+351 21 354 0465
→ p.32 Ⓕ

Gambrinus
R. das Portas de Santo
Antão 23
+351 21 342 1466
→ p.10 Ⓕ

MM Café
Av. Frei Miguel
Contreiras 52
teatromariamatos.pt
→ p.60 Ⓝ

Underdogs
R. Fernando Palha 56
+351 21 868 0462
under-dogs.net
→ p.48 Ⓒ

Under the Cover
R. Marquês Sá da
Bandeira 88B
underthecover.pt
→ p.31 Ⓢ

5. Other

Azenha do Mar
Azenha do Mar,
Odemira
+351 282 947 297
→ p.15, 56 Ⓕ

Cabrinha I
Beco do Bom Sucesso
4, Almada
+351 21 276 4732
cabrinha.com.pt
→ p.9 Ⓕ

Lisbon Oceanarium
Esplanada Dom Carlos
I, Parque das Naçoes
oceanario.pt → p.16 Ⓞ

Mar do Inferno
Av. Rei Humberto
II De Italia, Cascais
+351 21 483 2218
mardoinferno.com
→ p.55 Ⓕ

Piriquita II
R. das Padarias 18,
Sintra → p.32 Ⓕ

Restaurante Adraga
Praia da Adraga,
Colares
restaurantedaadraga.
com → p.15, 55 Ⓕ

**Restaurante Ponto
Final**
R. Ginjal 72
+351 21 276 0743
→ p.9, 33 Ⓕ

Available from LOST iN

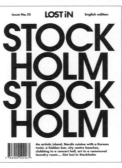

Next Issue: Copenhagen

WWW.LOSTIN.COM

Story

O Sapato

Gonçalo M. Tavares

A woman is confessing, and the words she is saying are prayers. It's already the time when the priest has forgiven her, and she's offering up several "Our Fathers". Too many, to be understandable—and there she is, non-stop, in continuous rotation, like a broken record, but one that does more than just repeat; sometimes there are variations of tone, of rhythm, slowdowns, accelerations, little hesitations in the repetition of the same word. Nevertheless, there are dozens and dozens of "Our Fathers" being said by a very beautiful woman, very attractive, who we now see has a beautiful neckline, yes, and also down there, by her kneeling legs we see she only has one shoe, only one, and she's missing the other. Where is that shoe? Let's look for it now as if the camera were well-behaved, as if it were elegant and delicate, some kind of boy scout that wants to do a good deed—there goes the camera looking for the shoe that is missing from the beautiful woman, the kneeling woman who does not stop praying in front of the confessional, but the truth is that even that beautiful song of confession that rings marvel-lously in this church of Lisbon, even that spiel can't lead the camera to the most important point—the point where we'd be satisfied after finding the sec-ond shoe, the shoe that's missing from that beautiful woman—and even without anything else, we'd end up with the feeling that everything was right and complete, because the second shoe would calm a certain discomfort and concern, but there's no damn second shoe, there's only one, and the second is not showing up, that second one that if it appeared would be an object and with it, it's true, would not appear the reasons for its separation from the first shoe, not even the narrative would be clarified, but it would be, even so, an object, a physical thing, the element of an addition that would complete a small part of the story, but the fact is the camera has done the good deed of a boy scout passing through the pews, and nothing—there's no extra shoe, all the other shoes are in their proper place, on the feet of the other believers distributed around the church,

praying: there are shoes, one on each side, and none missing. And, in fact, the church cannot solve the problem of anxiety, that is not the anxiety of the woman, but the anxiety of the camera that seeks to accelerate its movement in the search for the shoe, as if it were the camera missing a shoe and not the woman. But here it—the camera, not the woman—leaves breathlessly. Is it running late? Why is it leaving like that? The camera leaves the church, leaves the woman behind and runs, in a big hurry, as if it finally remembered something vital, as if it realised that it left something in the oven and has to run to prevent a fire, it is in such a hurry that it runs, that it runs at a tremendous speed; there it is then, the camera going around a building to run to the back of the building where there is a little grove and yes, there it moves the branches and pushes through the weeds, through the more or less tangled bushes and there it is, what is sought: the woman's shoe, the second shoe, finally and, yes, the process is con-cluded, the second shoe has been found and so the camera slows down, everything is peaceful now, and so now with extreme calm, with great slowness, the camera stops, quietly, in front of the dead boy next to the second shoe.

Born in Luanda in 1970, Gonçalo M. Tavares has won a sparkling array of awards for his novels, including the José Saramago prize for young writers for his novel "Jerusalém" and France's prestigious Best Foreign Book prize. Portuguese Nobel Laureate José Saramago said: "In thirty years' time, if not before, Tavares will win the Nobel Prize." Tavares' work has been published in more than 50 countries

LOST iN
FOUND OUT

Experience the city like a local

📍 **Insider recommendations**
Curated tips from creative locals

🗺 **Interactive map**
GPS your way to the choice spots

☁ **Download for offline use**
Wander free, without roaming

📋 **Create your itinerary**
Save your places, make your trip

LOST iN

 Download on the App Store

 GET IT ON Google Play

Reference Astronomical positions .... Trails

Boundary Lines — · — · —
shewn coloured thus — · — · —

ratma BG V
P T
Λ

Astronomical Positions

NAME OF PLACE	LATITUDE N.	LONGITUDE W. OF GREENWICH	AUTHORITY	NAME OF PLACE	LATITUDE N.	LONGITUDE W. OF GREENWICH	AUTHORITY
Punta Playa	8 33 22	59 59 48·5	1st Expedition	Camp 3 Cuyuni River	6 49 28·9	60 39 12·8	3rd Expedition
Mururuma River Mth	8 18 44	59 48 10	,, ,,	Camp 4 ,, ,,	6 47 04·8	60 46 36·3	,, ,,
Boundary Mark do	8 19 00	59 48 22·7	,, ,,	Ekerehu River Mouth	6 43 02·8	60 56 23·7	,, ,,
Mururuma River Hd	8 14 05·3	59 50 07·9	,, ,,	Wenamu River ,,	6 42 40·9	61 08 00·7	,, ,,
Haiowa River Mth	8 13 04	59 56 39·1	n ,,	Pathawaru Wenamu R.	6 28 02·3	61 07 54·1	4th Expedition
La Lancha, Amacura R.	8 02 18	60 05 00	,, ,,	Arawai Fall ,,	6 19 36·5	61 09 22·7	,, ,,
San Victor, ,,	7 58 42	60 10 05·5	,, ,,	Tshuau Village ,,	6 11 45·8	61 07 22·1	,, ,,
La Horqueta, ,,	7 52 18·2	60 18 22	,, ,,	Kura Falls ,,	6 03 42·5	61 16 46·6	,, ,,
Amacura River Hd	7 49 00	60 21 63·1	,, ,,	Dead Man's Camp ,,	5 58 06	61 22 55·7	,, ,,
Harrison Falls Barima R.	7 38 24	60 20 37·8	2nd Expedition	W most source Wenamu R.	3 56 55·4	61 23 24·7	,, ,,
Five Star Camp ,,	7 35 37	60 23 13·8	,, ,,	Paruima River Camp	5 51 01·7	61 03 08·1	,, ,,
Kaliaku Camp ,,	7 33 19	60 37 07·5	,, ,,	Kamarang ,, ,,	5 43 37·2	61 04 15·5	,, ,,
Barima River Head	7 28 24	60 41 31·2	,, ,,	Arriwe Matai	5 36 35	61 21 15·3	,, ,,
Akarabisi River Head	7 08 27·7	60 20 51·1	,, ,,	Yuruani River	5 11 00	60 58 36·5	,, ,,
,, Mouth	6 55 47·1	60 22 01·7	3rd Expedition	Kamaiwawong Village	5 10' 11·1	60 47 45·3	,, ,,
Camp 2 Cuyuni River	6 51 32·3	60 32 21·5	,, ,,	Boundary Mark Mount	5 10 09·6	60 45 58·2	,, ,,

Guyana in the World

Guyana
in the
World

The First of the
First Fifty Years
and
The Predatory
Challenge

Shridath Ramphal

HANSIB

First published in 2016 by Hansib Publications Limited
P.O. Box 226, Hertford, SG14 3WY
United Kingdom

info@hansibpublications.com
www.hansibpublications.com

ISBN 978-1-910553-59-6

A CIP catalogue record for this book
is available from the British Library

Produced by Hansib Publications Limited

"GUYANA remains resolute in defending itself against all forms of aggression. We remain wedded to the ideal of peace. We have never, as an independent state, provoked or used aggression against any other nation. We have never used our political clout to veto development projects in another country. We have never discouraged investors willing to invest in another country. We have never stymied development of another nation state. We do not expect, nor will we condone, any country attempting to do the same to us."

Extract from the Address by His Excellency Brigadier David Granger, MSS, President of the Cooperative Republic of Guyana to the 11th Parliament, Georgetown, on 9th July 2015

SHRIDATH Surendranath "Sonny" Ramphal, OE, OCC, served as Attorney General and Minister of Foreign Affairs of Guyana during the first decade of Guyana's Independence. He held the position of Secretary General of the Commonwealth from 1975 to 1990 where he was prominent in the struggle against UDI (Unilateral Declaration of Independence) in Zimbabwe and apartheid in South Africa. A committed regionalist, he headed the West Indian Commission which was tasked by CARICOM Heads of Government in 1990 to consult with the people of the Caribbean on a new direction for the integration movement. As the Region sought to consolidate its external trading arrangements, the CARICOM Regional Negotiating Machinery drew heavily on Sir Shridath's expertise and diplomacy with him as its first Chairman. Sir Shridath was a member of the Legal Team which advanced Guyana's case in the maritime boundary dispute with Suriname before an Arbitral Tribunal of the United Nations Convention on the Law of the Sea (2004 – 2007). He remains fiercely committed to the defence of Guyana's sovereignty and territorial integrity. He has authored several books some of which include *Glimpses of a Global Life* (2014), *Caribbean Challenges: Sir Shridath Ramphal's Collected Counsel* (2012), *Our Country, the Planet* (1992), *Inseparable Humanity* (1988), *One World to Share* (1979).

Preface

THIS small book, written at the request of Guyana's Ministry of Foreign Affairs, is intended as a contribution to the many publications that will mark the 50th Anniversary of our country's Independence attained on the 26th May 1966. I had the privilege to be Guyana's Attorney General at that time and to draft our Independence Constitution, including, as it did, clauses that later turned the country into the Republic of Guyana. It was to be changed again later, but that first occasion in 1966 gives our celebration in 2016 a special measure of pleasure for me.

That I was to be as well Guyana's Minister of State for External Affairs and later Foreign Minister, encouraged me to respond to the Ministry's wish, which was to recall Guyana's international experience in the early years of Independence. As we began to make our way in the world, though small and new to statehood, Guyana developed a record of contribution to world and regional affairs of which all Guyanese can be proud, and should be mindful at this time.

And there were other challenges that came with Independence. Prominent among them were predatory ones on our borders – challenges that continue to this day. They are challenges we have faced with valour and resolution, flying on our borders alongside the *Golden Arrowhead* the banner of peaceful resolution under the rule of international law. All Guyanese need to know the specifics of these threats. This time of renewal must contribute to that process.

In what follows, I have drawn on my memoire *Glimpses of a Global Life* and on my commentary *Triumph for UNCLOS.* I have relied, too, on the reflections of others: President David Granger's account *The Defence of the New River: 1967-1969,* Rudy Insanally's *Multilateral Diplomacy for Small States,* Odeen Ishmael's *The Trail of Diplomacy, Vols: 1-3*, Rashleigh Jackson's *Guyana Diplomacy* and Cedric Joseph's *Anglo-American Diplomacy and the Re-opening of the Guyana-Venezuela Boundary Controversy 1961-1966* – and to conversations with many of Guyana's diplomats. I am also much indebted to the late Joel Benjamin for his early researches.

To the Vice-President and Foreign Minister, Carl B. Greenidge, and the staff of the Foreign Ministry who have helped my efforts, to Elisabeth Harper and Rudolph Collins and to all the many others who have done so in varied ways, I acknowledge my gratitude.

SSR
26 May 2016

Contents

Commitment 5

Author 7

Preface 9

Foreword 13

PART 1

The First of the First Fifty Years

An Internationalist Guyana 17

Non-Alignment 22

Umana Yana 25

Cuba 29

The Caribbean Vineyard 33

Creating the ACP 46

PART 2

The Predatory Challenge

The Venezuelan Challenge 56

The Treaty of Washington, 1897 56

The Arbitral Tribunal 58

Venezuela applauds the Award 59

Demarcation of the Boundary 60

Venezuela protects the Boundary 62

Suriname's Questionings 65

The Boundary with Brazil 65

The Joint Boundary Commission 67

The Dutch join to fix the tri-junction point 67

Fixing the 'Northern Terminal' 72

Guyana's Independence stirs Suriname 73

Suriname's trespass in the New River area 74

Suriname aggression at sea 76

Recourse to International Law 79

Venezuelan greed revived 82

The Mallet-Prevost stratagem 83

The 'Cold War' dimension 84

The 'David and Goliath' torment 87

The Geneva Agreement, 1966 88

Fifty years of Venezuelan 'filibuster' 90

A clear path to 'judicial settlement' 92

Foreword

SIR Shridath is right to liken the first years of Independence to the experience of our young turtles on Shell Beach braving the hazards to reach the safety of the marine habitat beyond. For Guyana, it has been both brave and treacherous a passage and, at fifty years in our world journey, its insecurities are not yet wholly passed. This book is about that journey essentially from the perspective of Guyana's Ministry of Foreign Affairs, to which functional responsibility for that international interaction falls. In this Anniversary year, it seems right that we should share the experience, and particularly the achievements of Guyana in the world, no less than the threats we have encountered on our borders.

Guyana's Vice-President and Foreign Minister, Carl Greenidge

Part 1 is concerned with our global and regional encounters in the first of those first fifty years – encounters that were to shape the Guyana brand in world affairs, which the rest of those years were to see develop to its present fulfilment. We have been as internationalist as a small country can be, as globally enlightened as every member of our planetary community should be, as politically non-aligned as our circumstances dictate and as steadfast a member of the coterie of developing countries as solidarity demands. All this has characterised our foreign policy over these fifty years. And we have been the flag bearer of regionalism in all that time. There is much of which we should be proud in our encounters with the world.

Part 2 concerns achievement of another kind. The management of survival. On both our borders to the East and to the West, but much more ruthlessly so to the West, our neighbours have cast envious eyes on our patrimony – on land and at sea. In the case of Venezuela, despite the traditions of Bolivar, they walk in the footsteps of the colonizers and, like a new conquistador, would deny Guyana more than one-half of its territory. Their indifference to international law and 20th century global mores makes Guyana's cause that of all the world. It is necessary that their transgression of international values be known to the world. Our faith lies in the world – in the United Nations whose halls we entered fifty years ago.

I commend this account of *Guyana in the World* not only to all Guyanese but also to all who would know what small states can accomplish even in the face of continuing challenges to their survival with integrity.

Carl B. Greenidge
Minister of Foreign Affairs
Guyana

Part 1

The First of the
First Fifty Years

The First of the First Fifty Years

An Internationalist Guyana

THE First Fifty Years by itself would be a misleading sobriquet. It is apt only when understood as the first fifty years of the Independent State of Guyana that entered the world – the international community of States – as midnight ushered in the 26th of May 1966. It is really the 'last' fifty years that Guyanese are celebrating. Before them, in territorial continuity, was 'British Guiana', the Dutch colonies of Essequibo, Demerara and Berbice and, in the beginning, the 'wild coast' of South America, the unspoiled lands of our Amerindian people.

Kyk Over Al: Ruins in Guyana's Essequibo Region of Fort Kyk Over Al ("see over all") built by the Dutch in 1616 as guardian and symbol of sovereignty over the Dutch (later British) colony of Essequibo

That is our lineage. Those last fifty years were the first years of Independence, sealed formally the following September as the Prime Minister, Forbes Burnham, led Guyana's Delegation to our place in the General Assembly of the United Nations. That entrance, and the raising of the *Golden Arrowhead* among the flags of member States fluttering outside the General Assembly Building in New York, solemnised our entry into the world of States. It is with Guyana's early steps in those first fifty years in the world, and of the world, that this reflection is concerned. They were steps which marked our nation's formation and distinguished our country in the world. As Guyana turns *fifty,* they are years in that wider world which all Guyanese can recall with pride, and reflect on with resolve.

Despite the formalities, Independent Guyana was not entirely a newcomer to that world of States. The years preceding Independence had been turbulent on the domestic front and had brought British

Guyana entering the United Nations General Assembly

Cheddi Jagan and Forbes Burnham embarking for the world

Guiana ('B.G.') to the notice of the world – most notably through the struggle for independence led by Dr Cheddi Jagan in the environment of the 'cold war'. Through their international travels after Britain suspended British Guiana's Constitution in 1953, Dr Jagan and his then political partner, Forbes Burnham, made the Colony well known – in the UN and its agencies (the 'Decolonisation Committee' specially), in the Non-Aligned Movement, in the Commonwealth, in the Capitals of Africa and

Asia – and of the West, and in radical circles world-wide. When independent Guyana emerged in 1966, the new State was already well known to the world; and its own internationalism was full-blown. That head-start was to be significant in the fifty years that followed.

The late sixties and seventies were the years when the countries of the South, the 'Third World', made their first – and perhaps strongest – challenge for a just place in the post-colonial world. They were the years of political and intellectual struggle for a *New International Economic Order*, of 'North-South' contention on issues like a *Common Fund for Commodities,* on *Protectionism,* on *Reform of the Bretton Woods Institutions.* They were years that saw the rise of *South-South Cooperation,* resolute effort for a *Constitution for the Oceans,* the beginning of awareness of the *Threat to the Global Environment* and the *Vulnerability of Small States,* and even such seemingly esoteric (though crucial) issues as *the Definition of Aggression.* In all the relevant international fora (like UNCTAD and the Group of 77, and Committees of the General Assembly) and on all these issues, the new Guyana played a positive and respected role.

Guyana's diplomats were activist and held in high esteem; nowhere more so than at the United Nations where we were the first CARICOM country to be elected to the Security Council and to Chair it, and to the Presidency of the General Assembly – through Ambassadors Rashleigh Jackson and Rudy Insanally respectively. Meanwhile, Dr Mohammed Shahabudeen brought distinction to our Region as the first West Indian Judge of the International Court of Justice in The Hague.

But Guyana's roles were perhaps most prominent on the political front in leading the Caribbean on the African issues that dominated the seventies and eighties, namely *the Unilateral Declaration of Independence (UDI)* by the minority white regime of Ian Smith in Southern Rhodesia (now Zimbabwe) and *Apartheid* in South Africa. As Secretary-General of the Commonwealth for fifteen years, my personal contribution on these issues owed much to my Guyana roots. From those roots as well sprung Guyana's leadership roles in the UN's adoption of the *One China* policy in 1971 and our initiative in securing CARICOM's ending of the *Diplomatic Embargo against Cuba* in 1972. We were active too in relation to Namibia's freedom. Guyana was a member of the UN Council for Namibia from its inception in 1967 (a year after our Independence) and its President in 1974 – a position held with great distinction by Ambassador Rashleigh Jackson. During his Presidency the Council visited Guyana and it was on that occasion that the Monument of pillars of bull-forehead greenheart – dedicated to the *struggle for freedom everywhere* – was erected in Georgetown.

Guyana's first diplomats

The Liberation Monument

Non-Alignment

THE hosting of the Non-Aligned Foreign Ministers Meeting in 1972 was perhaps the high-water mark of Guyana's engagement with the international community, and tells the story of those activist times. It is wondrous to reflect that it was only six years after the country's independence. It deserves greater recall.

A major part of diplomatic life is the body of relationships that political leaders build up among themselves and sustain by their communication skills. Commonwealth Summits were especially suited to this purpose by virtue of the interactions they made possible, certainly in the time before their duration became truncated. They were particularly useful to the growing number of new developing country leaders making their global entrances. Guyana's first Commonwealth Summit was in September 1966 and our first Non-Aligned outing was in Lusaka, Zambia, in 1970, with Kenneth Kaunda as President. The 1966 Commonwealth Summit at which he and Prime Minister Burnham met was his first too; they were to meet again in 1969 at the next Commonwealth Summit in London. When in 1970 Kaunda chaired the Non-Aligned Summit in Lusaka, he ensured that Guyana should be the Meeting's Rapporteur.

By then, Guyana was prominent in the Caribbean in vigorous solidarity with Africa in the struggle against Ian Smith over his regime's 'UDI' (Unilateral Declaration of Independence) – an attempt to entrench minority white rule in Southern Rhodesia, and also in the wider struggle with South Africa over *apartheid*. What was most important, however, was that Kaunda knew that he had in Guyana a reliable friend and ally. And what was true of relations with Kenneth Kaunda was true for all the African 'Frontline States'. Tanzania's Julius Nyerere's relationship was as close; perhaps more intellectual, less emotional; but permeating it was the same confidence in a friend and ally. The point is, that in foreign policy issues of this kind, it is not only an articulated policy that matters; it is the personal confidence between leaders that gives the policy quality and substance.

At Lusaka, a Standing Committee of 16 Foreign Ministers was established to manage the Movement's affairs on an on-going basis. Not surprisingly, Guyana, the Rapporteur of the Lusaka Summit, was made a member. Within four years of Independence, Guyana was on the Executive of the worldwide Non-Aligned Movement. Ambassadors at the UN did the routine work of the Committee, but a meeting of the Committee at Foreign Ministers' level was required. Recognising that we could not aspire to ever hosting a Summit and that even a full Foreign Ministers' Meeting was probably beyond our capacity, the Government nevertheless agreed that hosting a Meeting of the 16-member Committee was something we could do, and that doing it would be good for Guyana. Our offer was accepted and in 1971 we hosted it – not on a grand scale, but efficiently.

It was not a good time in the Non-Aligned Movement. There was a major row over the seating of Cambodia under Prince Norodom Sihanouk's Government and over membership of the 'People's Revolutionary Government of South Vietnam' – with whom the Americans were at war. The latter issue, in particular, was incendiary with South-East Asian members like Indonesia, Singapore and Malaysia strongly opposed to the Non-Aligned Movement's position. And there was a fierce dispute between Algeria and Sri Lanka over the hosting of the next Non-Aligned Summit.

Ours was a two-day meeting and I chaired it as the host Minister. We were not expected to take decisions on the most contentious matters, but we had good discussions on them. Our last item was a decision on the venue of the forthcoming Foreign Ministers' Meeting the following year. There were no invitations on the table. Apparently, however, there had been conversations among the Foreign Ministers on the Committee, and a proposal came forward, without prior consultations with us, for the full Meeting to be held in Guyana. This was a genuine surprise. Sometimes such things are orchestrated, but this was not. We were genuinely astonished. We would be looking at a Conference of close to a hundred delegations. I asked for time to consult the Prime Minister and did so. Burnham asked whether we could do it, and at what cost? I said that almost certainly it would be beyond our means, judging by other such meetings – and probably beyond our capability as well. I warned also that there would be hemispheric sensitivities (thinking of Cuba's presence), but said that there would be big gains if we could manage it. His answer, typically decisive, was: *"Let's do it"*.

Umana Yana

IN Georgetown, near to a cluster of Government Departments and the City's then major hotel – the *Pegasus* – is a very large thatched cathedral-like building. It is a replica of an unusually large 'meeting place' of the *Wai Wai* tribe of Guyana's indigenous people. We chose it as the single structure we would build for the Meeting, and that we would have it erected in the manner of the *Wai Wai* with their forest materials, and by the tribe itself. Its construction was a major spectacle for city-folk; and the engineers among them were sceptical, for it went up without a nail. Yet, it remained in place for more than 40 years – as a monument to those who built it and our indigenous culture generally. We called it '*Umana Yana*' – the *Wai*

Umana Yana: in regional service

Wai words for 'meeting place of the people'. It was the central lounge of the Foreign Ministers' Meeting – where much of the work was done. Sadly, it was destroyed by fire a few years ago; but such a symbol it had become that the Government has had it re-built – and in the same fashion.

For the rest, we made do with what was there. The Pegasus could not accommodate all delegations but we made its ballroom the Plenary Hall of the Meeting. We asked Civil Servants in nearby departments to take their annual leave over the Meeting's duration; and we used the departments as Delegation and Committee Rooms. A private housing scheme of middle-income dwellings was nearing completion; and we were able to let delegations be the first occupants – with Georgetown housewives volunteering as house-mothers. We imported cars for use by Delegations and sold them immediately after at duty free prices – with no cost for their use to government. In these and other ways we managed. We had turned this exotic meeting of Non-Aligned Foreign Ministers into a community affair – not something happening outside the community. The Delegates responded to this community-style with great warmth, and for years after referred to it with appreciation. For our own part, we hoped it would give confidence to other small countries to host such occasions – within their means and cultures.

Umana Yana is not the only structural remembrance of the Conference. In the heart of Georgetown – in the much loved old 'Company Path Gardens' – we constructed a simple Memorial commemorating both the founders of the Movement and the holding of the Conference. It took the form of a collection of jasper boulders from the hinterland of Guyana set against the backdrop of a curved wall. Mounted on the wall are bronze busts of Egypt's Gamal Abdel Nasser, Ghana's Kwame Nkrumah, India's Jawaharlal Nehru and Yugoslavia's Josip Broz Tito. Set in the wall is a plaque bearing a

President Julius Nyerere at the Non Aligned Monument

dedication to these four men who more than any others inspired and shaped the early years of the Non-Aligned Movement. The busts were given by the respective Governments. They are I expect, the only such collection in the Western Hemisphere.

But of course the logistics of the Meeting were one thing; the politics of the agenda was quite another. Many thought that if the impasse over the 'Cambodia' and the 'South Vietnam' issues could not be resolved, the Movement would face dangers of self-destruction. Conscious of this, Guyana had developed a strategy to give the Meeting a substantial economic dimension drawing the meeting away from the traditional monopoly of political concerns, and guiding the Movement itself into greater preoccupation with economic development issues – which were in any event in the ascendancy on the international scene. To this end, we had convened a Group of Experts from Non-Aligned countries under the Chairmanship of the late William Demas, the respected economist from Trinidad and Tobago who then headed the CARICOM Secretariat in Georgetown. In developing and carrying forward this strategy we were helped by Yugoslavia and India in particular – old Non-Aligned hands.

The Expert Group had laboured hard in Georgetown before the Foreign Ministers' Meeting and had produced a draft Action Programme for Economic Co-operation among Non-Aligned Countries. This was to serve the world's developing countries well over many years as a core document on 'self-reliance'.

On the political issues there was vigorous and heated debate on some procedural issues. They were 'procedural' only in form; they had substantial 'cold war' overtones. They were, firstly, the upgrading of the status of the Provisional Revolutionary Government of South Vietnam (the North-backed forces) from 'Observer' to 'Member' of the Non-Aligned Movement. And second, the occupation by the delegation of the National Union of Cambodia (the Sihanouk delegation) of the Cambodia seat. Suffice it to say the meeting ended with the seating of the Delegation of the Provisional Revolutionary Government of South Vietnam as a member of the Non-Aligned Movement – and with inviting the Government of the National Union of Cambodia (Sihanouk) to occupy Cambodia's seat.

Within the Non-Aligned world, the Meeting was hailed as a great success for the Non-Aligned Movement – and for Guyana. There were many plaudits. I would have liked to say to many who were gracious what had been said to me before the Meeting began by the Foreign Minister of India. He was Sardar Swaran Singh, India's wise and respected Foreign Minister of many years. *"Young man"*, he had said, *"we will be electing you Chairman of this important Meeting. We do not expect you merely to occupy the Chair; we expect you to lead this Meeting. We will support you"*. I have chaired many an international meeting in the forty plus years since then. I have never forgotten Swaran Singh's wise counsel – or failed to follow it.

Cuba

THE Non-Aligned Meeting in Georgetown in 1972 had significance of many kinds; but there is one area that was – and is – very special to Guyana and the Caribbean. It is to do with Cuba. Inviting Cuba to the Meeting was never an issue with Guyana. Cuba was a member of the Non-Aligned Movement and would be invited and welcomed in the normal way. Besides, it had already been agreed by the Region that Cuba would participate in the first Caribbean Festival of Arts (CARIFESTA) due to be held in Guyana in the month after the Non-Aligned Meeting. Still, we were mindful that it would be the first fully international meeting in the Hemisphere that post-revolutionary Cuba would be attending outside the UN. Anti-Cuba sentiment was pervasive in Latin America as was adherence to the more formal diplomatic embargo under which, with the blessing of the Organisation of American States, the countries of the Hemisphere (with the exception of a principled Canada, Allende's Chile and an ambivalent Mexico) did not 'recognise' the Government of Cuba.

It was in this environment that, in inviting Cuba to attend the Foreign Ministers' Meeting, the Prime Minister had signalled to Havana (via our High Commissioner in Ottawa, where Cuba had an Embassy) that when their Foreign Minister came to Georgetown he would like to 'discuss' with him the matter of Guyana's diplomatic relations with Cuba. The Cuban Delegation was led by the experienced, if somewhat volatile, Foreign Minister, Dr Raúl

Greeting Cuba's Foreign Minister Raúl Roa

Roa. With him was Ambassador Ricardo Alarcon (later President of the Cuban National Assembly) with whom West Indian Missions at the UN had worked closely.

No sooner had I greeted Raúl Roa on his arrival at Timehri Airport than he intimated to me that, following on our signal through Ottawa, he had brought with him a draft 'Diplomatic Relations Agreement', and Plenipotentiary powers from President Fidel Castro to conclude it. We agreed to 'talk' in Georgetown. I needed time. Guyana was serious about 'diplomatic relations' with Cuba, but we had not contemplated formally establishing them at the Non-Aligned Meeting itself. We were already skating on thin diplomatic ice. I told Raúl Roa as much. He was understanding, but measured me quizzically. Was the signal from Georgetown 'diplomatic courtesy', he asked with his eyes? I assured him it was serious and substantive and that after the Meeting, and separate from it, we would conclude a Diplomatic Relations Agreement with Cuba.

In all this I was conscious of the national interests of Guyana, but I was conscious too of the interests of Caribbean integration. We were in the process of moving from 'first steps' CARIFTA to the more ambitious Community – to a Caribbean Community and Common Market (CARICOM). Two months away lay the Chaguaramas Summit at which such decisions would be taken by the Heads of the English-speaking Caribbean countries. I asked Raúl Roa to 'trust me'. Guyana, I told him, will establish diplomatic relations with Cuba, but we would prefer to give the three other independent English-Speaking Caribbean countries the chance to join us in doing so. *"Give me three months"*, I said, *"and we will have a multiple diplomatic relations agreement. That would be good for the Region, for Cuba and for Guyana; and it would make a dent in the hemispheric embargo"*.

Raúl Roa was disappointed, but he 'trusted' me; and for that I paid him tribute when I later reminisced on the event with Fidel Castro in Havana, when the West Indian Commission visited Cuba in 1992. Immediately after the Foreign Ministers' Meeting, Burnham contacted Trinidad and Tobago's Prime Minister, Eric Williams (the doyen of Caribbean Prime Ministers), Barbados' Prime Minister Errol Barrow (his old CARIFTA 'buddy'), and Michael Manley (his friend from London student days and newly elected Prime Minister of Jamaica). Ministers Kamaluddin Mohammed of Trinidad and Tobago and Dudley Thompson of Jamaica and Ambassador 'Boogles' Williams of Barbados (as an Observer) had been at the Meeting in Georgetown and were all briefed.

The 'Cuba' discussions in Georgetown were followed up with visits to the three Prime Ministers inviting them to join us in recognising Cuba – but making it clear that we were committed to doing so in any event. My itinerary was Kingston, Port of Spain, Bridgetown; Guyana's appeal was to justice, to history, to regional solidarity. The order of our approach was not haphazard; it reflected our judgment of the Prime Ministers most likely to agree. All three Prime Ministers agreed, and agreed further that their collective agreement, as Heads of Government of the independent English-speaking Caribbean countries, would be signalled when they met at Chaguaramas in Trinidad for a Summit meeting of the member-states of the Caribbean Free Trade Area – and so it was.

On 8 December 1972, I delivered on my promise to Raúl Roa when Oliver Jackman and Neville Selman signed the Diplomatic Agreement for Barbados and Guyana in Ottawa with Jose Fernandez (later Cuba's Ambassador in London); and Maxine Roberts and Eustace Seignoret signed for Jamaica and Trinidad and Tobago with Ricardo Alarcon at the UN in New York. The establishment of diplomatic relations with Cuba was announced simultaneously in all five Capitals. The effect of this sovereign collective Caribbean act of principle was immediate. The hemispheric diplomatic embargo of Cuba was not just dented; it collapsed. Today, Cuba has formal diplomatic relations with more than 190 countries.

On 8 December 2002, at a Cuba-CARICOM Summit arranged by President Fidel Castro, the then Prime Minister of Antigua and Barbuda, Lester Bird, quoted in his address from Pablo Neruda – the Chilean poet who won the Nobel Prize for Literature in 1971; words of which the Caribbean would be ever proud.

December 8th, 2002 was the 30th Anniversary of the signing of the Diplomatic Agreement between Cuba on the one hand and

CUBA APPEARS

"And so History teaches with her light
That man can change that which exists
And if he takes purity into battle
In his honour blooms a noble spring"

from
Pablo Neruda in Songs of Protest (1960)
(As quoted by former Prime Minister Lester Bird)

Barbados, Guyana, Jamaica and Trinidad and Tobago on the other. Eventually, other Caribbean English-speaking countries, when they became independent, followed the lead set by the original four. Today, 8 December each year is commemorated as Cuba-CARICOM Day. These were historic developments. Cuba has never forgotten the acts of solidarity, and courage, which they represented in those now far-off days of 1972. It was important also for Caribbean countries to reflect with Pablo Neruda that small as we are, we too once changed that which existed – and existed for much of the world – and all this, six years from 1966: in the sixth of our first fifty years of independence.

The Caribbean Vineyard

BUT in the early years of independence the new Guyana had other work to do in the world beyond our shores – but nearer home: work in our Caribbean homeland. As early as 1963, within a year of the dissolution of the Federation of the West Indies in which, shamefully, in my view, Guyana had not participated, and in an environment of resentment on all sides, Eric Williams, not the least of the contributors to acrimony, had taken an initiative to convene the First Conference of the Heads of Government of the Commonwealth

Caribbean – only four Heads, the Prime Ministers of Jamaica and Trinidad and Tobago and the Premiers of Barbados and Guyana.

Dr Williams, at that first Conference, pointed to a need which Independence on an island basis could not solve: the need to unite in the face of other emerging economic groupings. He said:

> *"As our countries achieve Independence or proceed to Independence, we enter into a world dominated increasingly by regional Groupings, both economic and political. Western Europe has succeeded. Africa is succeeding and efforts are being made to translate the political association in the Western Hemisphere into regional economic Groupings – the Latin American Free Trade Area and the Central American Common Market. Small countries like ours encounter great difficulty in establishing their influence in a world dominated by power and Regional Associations".*

These compulsions were to drive Caribbean economic integration for years to come; but Dr Williams advanced no proposals for meeting them.

The mood, however, was changing. The case for Caribbean economic cooperation, at least, was palpable. Less than two years later, with his old friend Burnham now in office in Guyana, Errol Barrow in Barbados initiated action towards establishing a free trade area between the two countries in the first instance, and the rest of the Caribbean at such time as they would be ready to join. I was only just on the scene in Guyana as Attorney-General. Having recently done my Master's dissertation on *West Indian Federalism* it was time enough to become involved in drafting what was to become the Caribbean Free Trade Area Agreement – CARIFTA.

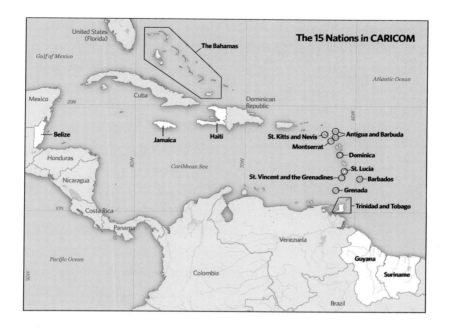

The 15 Nations in CARICOM

With Antigua joining, it was signed at Dickenson Bay, Antigua, in 1965. When the CARIFTA Agreement actually became operational in 1968, eleven Caribbean countries had become signatories. The rebuilding of regionalism had begun – this time, with Guyana in a lead role.

The decade that followed – the first years of Guyana's Independence – was one of extraordinary Caribbean vision and action, regionally and beyond the Region: a time which has not been replicated since, save in spasms of enlightenment. But in Guyana in those early years, we believed that there existed a new and favourable climate for West Indian unity. With CARIFTA everything had changed. The ice that had hardened over West Indian unity with the dissolution of the Federation had, at last, been broken. The dialogue that had started with the Caribbean Heads of

Government Conferences in 1963 now had an agenda of action. And with that came the rest – sensitivity to the new mood of the area, an understanding of each other's special problems and a tolerance with each other's actions. Above all, we began to suppress suspicion and to act again like members of a family. True, we were to have many an argument about 'co-operation' and 'integration'. And it was not always a semantic one. Nor is it wholly over.

Errol Barrow and Forbes Burnham were both committed West Indians for whom economic integration needed no advocacy. Even so, in approaching CARIFTA initially, their emphasis was slightly different. Barrow had given up in deep frustration on the 'Little Eight' – the effort to salvage mechanisms of unity between Barbados and the seven Leeward and Windward islands – helped (as he was) by Sir Arthur Lewis, St Lucia's Economics Nobel Laureate. His main aim now was to enlarge Barbados' 'domestic' market; Guyana was the most likely candidate; perhaps, even Antigua whose Premier, V.C. Bird, was a trusted friend; Trinidad and Tobago, with its greater manufacturing capacity, would be counter-productive. Burnham's vision was larger, more political, and less immediately economic. A start, he felt, had to be made in rebuilding regionalism and, with Barrow in office, the Barbados-Guyana axis was reliable, as was Antigua under 'V.C.' Bird.

A Free Trade Agreement between Antigua, Barbados and British Guiana – (CARIFTA) – inspired by Barrow, developed by Burnham and hosted by V.C. Bird was a microcosm of unity; but it was a practical revival of regionalism. Burnham's idea never was a CARIFTA of three, and having engineered the deferral of the coming into force of the Agreement for a year (against Barrow's inclination), it fell to Guyana to lead the effort to bring the others on board – particularly Jamaica and Trinidad and Tobago. The legwork to secure this was Guyana's. It was not exactly easy.

There were some who felt at the time that CARIFTA was a precipitate step and, far from marking the re-emergence of unity, would set back a new start. Indeed, as late as 1967 there were rumblings of this kind from more than one West Indian Capital. But Burnham was not dismayed; he had taken a calculated risk, and such reactions were within his calculations. What Guyana had done was to give notice of an intention to proceed with CARIFTA – and we were certain that before the Free Trade Area actually started the movement toward unity would develop momentum. Moreover, we had deliberately given time for this development by retarding the start of the Free Trade Area – even at the vexation of initial colleagues.

When Eric Williams decided that this was not an invitation for Trinidad and Tobago to turn down, and when the six Leeward and Windward Islands (by then States in Association with Britain but responsible for all their affairs except external relations and defence) came on board, it did not take long for Jamaican manufacturers to persuade the country's pragmatic Trade Minister, Robert Lightbourne, that Jamaica should not stand aloof – or for him, as Trade Minister of the region's largest economy, to persuade his colleagues, in an anti-regional Government, that regionalism after all had a plus side. When the CARIFTA Agreement actually became operational in 1968, eleven Caribbean countries had become signatories. The rebuilding of regionalism had begun. And, this time, Guyana was in the forefront.

We believed, in Guyana, that there existed a new and favourable climate for West Indian unity. No one could be sure exactly what patterns that unity might take and, certainly, we did not attempt to draw up blueprints at that stage of transition when so many new constitutional relationships were just being established. But, that there was now a climate propitious to regionalism we felt certain.

If we were to be responsive to it and sensitive to the many and changing moods of the area; if we all tried harder to understand the special problems of our several countries and to be tolerant of each other's behaviour in the search for solutions to them; if, above all, we could suppress suspicion and replace silence by dialogue, there was perhaps much that we might yet achieve that had eluded the West Indies for so long.

There are few things in life that are the result of pure accident, and Governments cannot proceed on a philosophy of vacuous expectation of something turning up. Much work was done in quiet patient ways in the years before a refined CARIFTA became operational. As a result, when the Fourth Commonwealth Caribbean Heads of Government Conference convened in Barbados in October 1967, a climate for West Indian unity was found in fact to exist and it was possible for agreement to be reached on the important resolutions of that meeting – resolutions that have since shaped the programme of regional economic integration.

In 1970, Dr Williams inscribed *From Columbus to Castro* to me – *"My dear Sonny, we are both labourers in the vineyard. It is in this spirit that I send you this book"*. It was a time of expectation. The Caribbean Community and Common Market was on its way to being agreed. The vineyard was being planted, and the labour of nurturing would continue. Work on the Treaty to formalise and fill it out was in hand under the guidance of Demas and his colleagues at the Secretariat, inspiring a generation of regionalists – economists and others. The Treaty was signed at Chaguaramas on 4 July 1973 – the original Treaty of Chaguaramas – signed initially by Prime Ministers Errol Barrow, Forbes Burnham, Michael Manley and Eric Williams – a signing described as *"a landmark in the history of the West Indian people"*; and so it was!

Signing of the Treaty of Chaguaramas, 4 July 1973

I have dwelt upon these beginnings for two reasons. First, because it is good to recognise how much had been achieved in the years after Dickenson Bay. Second, because it is necessary to take note of the lessons of the early years in determining the patterns of action in the years ahead – in particular, the lesson that progress will follow if courage and inventiveness lead the way. Guyana, this time, was on the right side of history.

The Free Trade Area had been established and the Council of Ministers that charted its course had begun, through its quarterly meetings, to function in pragmatic ways, substituting practicality for dogma and acknowledging the inevitability of compromise and concession. The Regional Secretariat under the eminent leadership of William Demas – had begun to establish an identity of its own and to put into high gear the machinery of integration. The Charter of the Regional Development Bank was signed by all the parties by the end of 1969, the target date Guyana had suggested at the Heads of Government Conference in Trinidad earlier that year. It was a target met despite the doubts of those who felt we were pushing rather too hard; that we were running risks with the establishment of the Bank in order to meet an unrealistic deadline. Suffice it that the Bank was established and that we were able to start the 1970s with this important trinity – CARIFTA, the Regional Secretariat and the Regional Development Bank – established and functioning. So prominent was Guyana's leadership in these years that it was accepted almost as a matter of course that Georgetown should host the Headquarters of CARIFTA – the Regional Secretariat.

Many contributed to this achievement including others besides Governments – particularly the voluntary organisations, groups like the Incorporated Commonwealth Chambers of Commerce and Industry of the Caribbean, like trade union organisations throughout the region, like manufacturers' associations everywhere, like the media of the region – all helped by their own enthusiasm to carry the movement along; they all deserved of the region its gratitude.

Still, we had barely laid the foundations of Caribbean integration. Very much more remained to be done; and it is well that, at the beginning of the 1970s, we should have set our perspectives and understood the enormity of the undertaking ahead. Guyana recognised that it had to be for the Caribbean a decade of decision – a decade that would settle, perhaps this time for all time, whether we move on in ever narrowing circles to unity in cohesion, or spin off into separate orbits like so many wayward stars lost in the constellation of the world community. What were some of these decisions for which Guyana called?

We had to decide, first of all, to consolidate the new institutions that had been established, and to ensure that they worked as instruments of integration. CARIFTA, the Secretariat and the Caribbean Development Bank are instruments of integration. As instruments, they have to be used – and used by West Indians – if they are to make economic integration a reality.

Guyana believed that our future must be bound up with agriculture to a very large degree; and we were certain – and said so – that CARIFTA would fail to achieve its goals of promoting the integration of the economies of the region unless we could demonstrate that there was in it a place for the primary producers of the region; unless we could demonstrate effectively that CARIFTA was something more than a confederation of manufacturers' associations. We wanted to secure for its implementation the same enthusiasm and practical support that had already been given to the establishment of the free trade arrangements at the level of manufactured products. It was particularly necessary that this enthusiasm and support should be demonstrated and given in the bigger countries; for from CARIFTA itself the Associated States (the smaller islands) had little to gain unless the Agricultural Marketing Protocol worked effectively. We knew that they were looking to see whether it was the intention that CARIFTA should work for them too.

We needed also to consolidate the Regional Secretariat. In making William Demas available as its Secretary-General, the Government of Trinidad and Tobago had demonstrated the importance it attached to integration, and set a notable standard of self-sacrifice for other West Indian Governments – not all of whom had been willing to make corresponding gestures to the success of regional institutions. Guyana saw the Regional Secretariat emerging in the 1970's as a central agency for regional action, working closely with the Regional Development Bank but having a wide area of activity that went well beyond economic development in its narrowest sense. We saw the Shipping Council and the 'Regional Carrier', the Universities and the Examinations Council, all coordinated at the regional level within the Secretariat; and we saw the Secretariat, through this role of co-ordination, helping to fashion the programme of integration that Governments would promote. Guyana worked with Demas' great successor, Alister McIntyre (now Sir Alister), to further these integration goals.

And perhaps, as great as anything else, was the need to consolidate the Regional Development Bank as a West Indian institution. Although 40 per cent of the Bank's equity was contributed by non-regional Governments, we believed that none would say that their contribution was anything other than a contribution towards making this vital West Indian institution an effective instrument of integration and of West Indian economic development more generally. Guyana led the effort to enshrine this philosophy.

In Guyana's vision of the 1970s we saw in the skies of the Caribbean, and beyond, a regional airline staffed by West Indians and flying a regional banner. We saw, too, in the seas of the Caribbean, and beyond, a West Indian shipping service providing a more effective sea link within the region than we had and, through extra-territorial services to our principal trading ports outside the region, freeing us from arbitrarily manipulated freight rates that could have so crippling an effect on that economic development towards which our other efforts were directed. Work of this kind was in hand within the Secretariat with assistance from the University of the West Indies and agencies of the United Nations. That work included attention to a common external tariff; a location of industries policy; harmonisation of fiscal incentives, and a regional fishing policy – to identify the most prominent. It was a monumental process, but undertaken at all levels from Heads of Government down with an astonishing measure of regional commitment given all that preceded it in the years before 1965.

In the decade that followed – and particularly in the 1970s – all the matters I have outlined, and more, engaged the attention of regional Ministers under the overall policy decisions of regional Prime

"Integrate or Perish"

"Either we weld ourselves into a regional grouping, serving primarily Caribbean needs, or lacking a common positive policy, have our various territories and states drawn hither and thither into, and by, other large groupings, where the peculiar problems of the Caribbean are lost or where we become the objects of neo-colonialist exploitation and achieve the pitiable status of international mendicants....

This is the naked truth. Either we integrate or we perish, unwept, unhonoured."

Prime Minister Forbes Burnham, 14 August, 1967

Ministers (there were no Presidents yet). Guyana spoke to them and cerebrated on them – always with a regional outlook. In due course, these multitudinous deliberations led to an essential clutch of practical Agreements.

And as important as anything we did in those years was Guyana's articulation of the policy of regional integration and the philosophy of Caribbean oneness that would sustain it. In January 1973, for example, speaking for Guyana to the Royal Commonwealth Society in London on *"The Prospect for Community in the Caribbean"*, I said:

> *"You will appreciate from all I have said that in these first years of our own independence, the Caribbean has been for Guyana an area of concentration. Our immediate pre-occupation is to implement the decisions taken last October for the establishment of the Caribbean Community, including the Caribbean Common Market. Our objective is to maximise the economic strength of the Region. Our vision is that of West Indian Nationhood. I like to think that we have made some amends for defaults of a decade ago".*

The point is that in these years of activism in the cause of West Indian unity Guyana never tired in its furtherance. It was a task that would never end.

In the evolution of CARIFTA and CARICOM there were many players over many years by Guyana's side. We were by no means alone. Some of those who worked at the furnace of those meetings in Georgetown that changed the fortunes of the integration process, should not be forgotten. Premiers like Robert Bradshaw of St Kitts and Edward LeBlanc of Dominica, pioneering Ministers like Antigua's Lester Bird, Grenada's Derek Knight, Jamaica's Robert Lightbourne, St Lucia's George Mallet, St Vincent's James 'Son' Mitchell, Trinidad and Tobago's Kamaluddin Mohammed, St Kitts' Paul Southwell and Lee Moore, Jamaica's P. J. Patterson, and Barbados' Branford Taitt – and they were only some of those whose labours paved the way for CARICOM – all sustained at meetings in Guyana (as those who attended will recall) by Mrs Ting-a-Kee's 'crab-backs' – and much more. And the CARIFTA Secretariat itself – with William Demas and Alister McIntyre combining world-class professionalism with passionate regionalism – was not a passive agency, keeping the records. On the contrary, the Secretariat drove the process, and by their dynamism and technical excellence inspired it.

It took all this and more, including camaraderie at all levels among decision-makers – camaraderie that took many forms besides solidarity around the conference table – many forms of togetherness of which friendships were built and confidences strengthened. Sailing in the Grenadines, duck shooting in Guyana, feasting on curried goat in Antigua, not to mention carnival and cricket and carousing on ferry boats on the Demerara River – all this too was part of the story of CARIFTA and its transition to CARICOM – and it was very much a Guyana story.

And the story continued beyond economic integration to the realisation of the cultural affinities which were at the core of West Indian identity. In 1972 – the same year that Georgetown was the venue of the Non-Aligned Foreign Ministers Meeting – we hosted the first ever Caribbean Festival of Arts – *CARIFESTA '72*. It was at once a celebration of Caribbean cultural identity and a spectacular display of Caribbean variety within oneness. And it was the Caribbean beyond CARICOM. Cuba was here; and so were the Dutch and French-speaking territories. It was another beginning the young Guyana generated for its regional homeland. And *CARIFESTA* flourishes!

The journey from CARIFTA to Community has been well chronicled by William Demas in '*From CARIFTA to CARICOM*'. One of the lessons the journey teaches is the importance, sometimes the essentiality, of starting on a regional course, even if only a few in the region are ready to begin the journey. This may be valid in many contexts; it has a compelling logic in the context of our

Carifesta'72
Caribbean Festival of Creative Arts
GEORGETOWN, GUYANA
Aug. 25 — Sept. 15, 1972

scattered archipelago. Where would we have been had CARIFTA not been started in 1965? Where would we have been without the Guyana of the first of our fifty years of Independence?

In an interdependent world, which in the name of liberalisation makes no distinctions between rich and poor, big and small, unity is a Caribbean compulsion. West Indian states – for all their separate flags and anthems – need each other for survival, the way villages do within a wider whole. With village affairs under 'local control' they could experiment with non-political forms of cooperation; and this they did after the more ambitious federal project was abandoned by some and lost to others. The leadership later came from Guyana – alas, too late – where the vision of an integrated West Indian people loomed large with a new political dispensation carrying none of the baggage of 'federation'. It was a dispensation that allowed Guyana space and a supportive environment to push on the new boundaries of unity.

Creating the ACP

TO say that the seeds of the Lomé Convention were sown on the lawns of the Guyana Prime Minister's residence in Georgetown is perhaps going too far; but there is more than a grain of truth in it. It was 1972 and the Caribbean was not only preparing to advance from CARIFTA to CARICOM within the region, but also to venture forth into Europe. I was involved in each process as Guyana's functional Foreign Minister. But more important than any one person – was Guyana.

The first thing to note about those times was Guyana's relative freshness and creativity. 1973 was a time of awareness of the need for a wider unity. Developing countries had found strength in their new spirit of oneness at the level of the G77, and confidence in their global pursuit of a new order – primarily a new international economic order. At the United Nations in New York, at UNCTAD in Geneva, in international gatherings around the world the theme of the South was 'unity'; and in the North-South dialogue that dominated the global scene developing countries gave intellectual leadership at diplomatic and technocratic levels.

Nowhere was that regional unity more manifest than in the negotiations with Europe for a new post-colonial trade and economic regime – the process which became known as the 'Lomé negotiations', taking its name from the Capital of Togo where it was signed. Caribbean countries played a leadership role – politically and professionally – in those negotiations between the fledgling European Community of nine members and their erstwhile colonies in Africa, the Caribbean and the Pacific. So far as the Caribbean was concerned, they were negotiations effectively compelled by Britain's membership of the Community.

Guyana was the Caribbean's spokesman for the negotiations – chosen by regional Governments. Our policy positions in the negotiations would be shaped by the Region; but these were

The ACP logo designed for the Georgetown meeting, 1975

negotiations in which we would be interacting with African and Pacific countries. It was obvious that securing the maximum degree of unity possible with them was going to be important. Perhaps, I thought, this was a good moment to begin the process of exploring the possibilities of unity. So, shortly before the Foreign Ministers met, I told my colleagues on the CARIFTA Council of Ministers the following:

> *"I intend to make use of the meeting of Non-aligned Foreign Ministers in Guyana to talk with all our colleagues from the Commonwealth about the EEC. I hope that we can involve all our colleagues from the Caribbean in those discussions. These are not formal discussions. They are not secret discussions. They are just talks to see if we can get other people to pool their resources with ours in relation to the negotiations that lie ahead."*

To this end, Prime Minister Burnham allowed his Reception to accommodate a meeting of relevant Ministers in a short discussion on the upcoming negotiations with Europe. It was a large Reception and we were able without disruption to corral the particular Ministers into a nearby room for the discussion. We ensured that our principal technicians, like Alister McIntyre were on hand. It was the evening of 9 August 1972 and I have been reminded since that on those lawns we were almost equidistant from Africa to the East and the Pacific Islands to the West.

That informal discussion was the beginning of a process that led eventually to the pooling of the resources of all the African, Caribbean and Pacific States – 'Associates' and 'Associables', 'French-speaking' and 'English-speaking', 'AASM' and 'Commonwealth Members' – in the negotiations with the EEC that ended in the Lomé Convention. It was the beginning – though we did not know it then – of the ACP. In September 1972, Caribbean Officials visited East and West Africa apprising their colleagues of Caribbean preparations and paving the way for Ministerial Meetings in Lagos, Nairobi, Abidjan, Georgetown, Dar es Salaam, Dakar, Kingston and Accra.

From that time onward there was no turning back to separateness. At the next joint ACP/EEC Ministerial meeting in Brussels in October 1973, the ACP case presented by three voices in July was now urged by one voice – that of the then current Chairman of the African Group. This was in response to a specific Caribbean offer made by Guyana that the demonstrated unity of the ACP Group be symbolised and formalised by such a single presentation. Thereafter, throughout the discussions, extending over a year, the ACP never negotiated otherwise than as a Group and spoke always with one voice. It was often an African voice, sometimes a Caribbean or a Pacific voice; but always a voice that spoke for the ACP.

The unity of interests of the ACP became more manifest as the negotiations lengthened and, as was dramatically revealed in the ultimate stages when, rum, a product of interest to only one region – the Caribbean – threatened to frustrate the eventual consensus. Neither regional nor linguistic affinities, neither separate national interests nor past associations, neither personalities nor cultural patterns, were allowed to supersede the interest of the Group as a whole. Rum was a Caribbean product. Africa – Francophone and Anglophone – was willing to forego its hard won gains in the negotiations if the Caribbean's needs on rum were not met. They made that clear to Europe. Caribbean needs were met. For me, that was the finest moment in the negotiations; for it was a moment of solidarity that had truly begun on the Prime Minister's lawns in Georgetown two years before.

The Lomé Convention was not perfect; but it was a point of departure in the relations between the developing and the developed States. The negotiations were then the most effective negotiations on a package of comprehensive economic arrangements ever conducted by developing countries with any major sector of the developed world. That it was such an innovation and represented such a promise derived in the main from the process of unification described above; it was a process that brought together what were then 46 developing States in a uniquely effective manner to meet the challenge of negotiating with the European Economic Community – a significant segment of the developed world that had itself so rightly turned to integration in answer to the challenge of survival. The Lomé Convention was to last for 20 years – renewed three times with improvement.

Guyana took satisfaction in the conclusion of the Lomé Convention; but more in the evolution of the ACP – by now, the largest inter-continental group of developing countries working in functional unity. To consummate this Guyana invited the Ministers of the ACP, who had bonded through the negotiations, to meet in Georgetown to formally establish the ACP in its own right. In June 1975 – at what was to be my last Conference as Foreign Minister – the ACP Ministers signed the '*Georgetown Agreement*' establishing the ACP with objectives beyond the implementation of the Lomé Convention.

The ACP now has its own Headquarters in Brussels. I was pleased that on 12 February 2009 the European Commission honoured Hon. P J Patterson, the distinguished former Prime Minister, and previously Trade Minister, of Jamaica and me by the naming of a special room in the EU Headquarters in Brussels after us – for our *"historic contribution to Caribbean-European co-operation"*. Jamaica had partnered Guyana in guiding the negotiations to their conclusion.

LA CONVENTION DE LOMÉ IV (1990)

R. GIMENO, P. MITRANO, novembre 1999

Caraïbes :
• Bahamas
• Barbade
• Grenade
• Trinidad et Tobago
• Dominique
• Sainte-Lucie
• Antigua-et- Cap-
  Barbuda   Vert
• Saint-
  Christophe
  et Nièves
• Saint-Vincent
  et les
  Grenadines

Sao Tomé et •
Principe

Afrique

Pacifique :
• Fidji
• Tonga
• Samoa Occidentales
• Kiribati
• Iles Salomon
• Tuvalu
• Vanuatu

• Seychelles
• Comores

SCIENCES PO
cartographie

Maurice

Pays de la CEE et ACP
(Afrique Caraïbe Pacifique)
ayant ratifié la convention

Afrique du Sud : membre à statut
restreint depuis le 24 avril 1997.

Sources : *Commission européenne,
Direction générale du Développement, 1997.*

Projection J. Bertin

The ACP-EEC countries of the Lomé Convention

None of this would have been possible without the progress we were making at home in developing the fledgling CARIFTA structures into the much larger, more ambitious framework of Community. Indeed that evolution of the 'CARICOM' negotiations proceeded side by side with the negotiations with Europe. Before we journeyed to Lomé in February 1975, four Caribbean countries had journeyed first to Chaguaramas in July 1973 to sign the Treaty establishing the Caribbean Community. Within a year, another eight of the present member States (except the Bahamas) had joined the group. These processes of ambitious activism at home and abroad were mutually reinforcing. It helped us abroad that we were working together at home; it helped us at home that we were working effectively abroad. Neither was without difficulty, for all that. But in each area of effort it became easier to overcome.

The second compelling lesson is how critical it was to pool our resources – political, economic and intellectual – in negotiating with countries beyond ourselves: globally, in Europe, in the

Hemisphere, and within the wider Caribbean. As regards the Lomé negotiations, the process of unification – for such it was – added a new dimension to the Third World's quest for economic justice through international action. Its significance, however, derives not mainly from the terms of the negotiated relationship between the 46 ACP States and the EEC, but rather from the methodology of unified bargaining which the negotiations pioneered. Never before had so large a segment of the developing world negotiated with so powerful a grouping of developed countries so comprehensive and so innovative a regime of economic relations. It was a new, and salutary, experience for Europe; it was a new, and reassuring, experience for the ACP States. And Guyana, that played so prominent a role in the process, had travelled only six of the fifty years we have now done.

It is worthy of note that as we celebrate our 50th Anniversary of Independence, a Guyanese diplomat, Ambassador Patrick Ignatius Gomes, occupies the office of Secretary General of the ACP in Brussels.

Part 2

The Predatory
Challenge

The Predatory Challenge

ON Guyana's north-western shore – the Essequibo Coast – is *Shell Beach*. It is the quintessence of Guyana itself in its need for protection of the new born turtles that rise from its golden sands only to battle their way to survival past predators in their path. Guyana's first fifty years have been like the first hazardous moments of our turtles. And as it is with them, it has been and remains the world's responsibility to secure new-born countries like Guyana from the predators that would devour them. The world seeks to discharge that responsibility essentially by international law. It is by violating international law that others on their frontiers try to despoil them of the right to survival that is their patrimony. So has it been with Guyana. And as fifty years are but an hour in a nation's life, that threat to survival persists.

Newborn turtles at Shell Beach, Essequibo

The Venezuelan Challenge

THE process of decolonisation is for many the greatest achievement of the post-war world, and Guyana's Independence was a part of it. It was a process welcomed by most freedom loving people and Governments. But the welcome of Guyana's freedom was not shared by the Government of its neighbour to the west who, ironically, was to call their country *the Bolivarian Republic of Venezuela*. That singular aversion to Guyana's freedom was the very converse of all that Simon Bolivar symbolises. And it was not resentment alone that Venezuela nurtured. In anti-Bolivarian fashion, Venezuela actually tried to obstruct Guyana's Independence – to prevent the start of the last fifty years. This could not be the wish or the work of our brothers and sisters in Venezuela, the ordinary people of our neighbouring land. They are neighbours against whom the people of Guyana nurture no ill will. But there are classes and forces in Venezuela that have made the acquisition of most of Guyana their life's cause, and sought to turn it into a national crusade – Venezuela, already the fifth largest country of South America, with Guyana among the smallest.

The Treaty of Washington, 1897

AS early as 1962, four years before Guyana's Independence, the then Venezuelan Government had taken advantage of Guyana's pending freedom to try to reopen with Britain a long-settled border controversy involving more than half of Guyana's land area. It was a spurious and, in some ways, a sinister contention; and this was their second effort to rob Guyana of its patrimony. Three months before Guyana's Independence, in early 1966, Britain invited the 'about to be independent' Guyana to join in its conversations with Venezuela in the hope that the new country could be rid of

Venezuelan greed at birth. The outcome was the Geneva Agreement between Venezuela and the United Kingdom, to which on attaining independence, Guyana became a party 'in addition to' Britain. It was our first international foray; and Prime Minister Burnham and I attended. I am, perhaps, the only one on any side at Geneva, who is alive on Guyana's fiftieth birthday.

That Meeting in Geneva should not have been necessary, for Guyana's boundary with Venezuela had been formally settled over a hundred years previously by an International Tribunal of Arbitration under a Treaty freely signed by Venezuela and ratified by its Congress.

President Joaquin Crespo commending the Treaty of Washington to the Venezuelan Congress on 20 February 1897 for ratification

"It is eminently just to recognise the fact that the great republic (the United States of America) has strenuously endeavoured to conduct this matter in the most favourable way, and the result obtained represents an effort of intelligence and good will worthy of praise and thanks from us who are so intimately acquainted with the conditions of this most complicated question. It is your duty according to the constitutional law of the republic to examine the treaty which the Venezuelan Minister Plenipotentiary signed in accordance with the bases referred to and the change proposed by the executive power in regard to the formation of the arbitral tribunal. And as this is an affair of such importance involving as it does such sacred interests, I beg you that from the moment it is presented for your consideration you will postpone all other business until you shall decide upon it. (translation).

Venezuela had long cast envious eyes on the Essequibo region of Guyana – some two-thirds of Guyana. Britain claimed in turn the Orinoco Delta of oil rich Venezuela. It was the days of the Monroe Doctrine and the United States, acting as Venezuela's patron, had

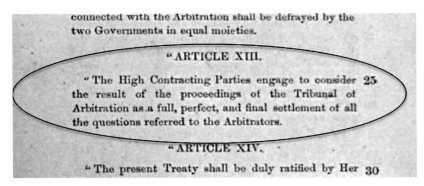

connected with the Arbitration shall be defrayed by the
two Governments in equal moieties.

"ARTICLE XIII.

"The High Contracting Parties engage to consider 25
the result of the proceedings of the Tribunal of
Arbitration as a full, perfect, and final settlement of all
the questions referred to the Arbitrators.

"ARTICLE XIV.

"The present Treaty shall be duly ratified by Her 30

The Treaty of Washington, 1897

pressured Britain into agreeing to signing the Treaty of Arbitration
with Venezuela under threat of war – so fierce was America's
hemispheric posture. That was 2nd February 1897. It was a Treaty
to settle for all time the Boundary between Venezuela and Britain's
colony of British Guiana. Venezuela and Britain undertook in
solemn terms *"to consider the results of the proceeds of the Tribunal
of Arbitration as a full, perfect and final settlement of all the
questions referred to the Arbitrators"*.

The Arbitral Tribunal

VENEZUELA claimed that they were the heirs of Spanish
colonialism and that Spain had occupied more than half of the
British colony before the British came. The Tribunal went into the
most elaborate examination of the history of the occupation of the
territory. The arguments took four hours each day, four days each
week and covered a period of nearly three months. The verbatim
records of the hearings occupy 54 printed volumes – with cases
and counter-cases, and additional documents, correspondence and
evidence. The Tribunal was presided over by M. de Martens,
Professor of International Law at the University of St Petersburg,
perhaps the most eminent international lawyer of the time. The
other judges were: on the part of Venezuela, US Chief Justice Weston

> ## Rules of Procedure of the Tribunal of Arbitration, Rule XXIV
>
> **The final award, duly declared and communicated to the Agents of the two Governments being in dispute shall be deemed to decide definitely the points in dispute between the Governments of Great Britain and of The United States of Venezuela concerning the lines of their respective frontiers, and shall finally close all Proceedings of the Tribunal of Arbitration established by the Treaty of Washington.**

Fuller, nominated by the President of Venezuela; Justice David Josiah Brewer, of the US Supreme Court, nominated by the President of the United States and, on the part of Great Britain, Lord Russell of Killowen (Lord Chief Justice of England) and Sir Richard Henn Collins, a Lord Justice of Appeal of the English High Court. It is these four Judges that together chose Professor de Martens as the President of the Tribunal.

Venezuela applauds the Award

ON 3 October 1899, the International Tribunal of Arbitration presented its Award. In the words of the law firm handling Venezuela's case, written in the American Journal of International Law as late as 1949: *"The Award secured to Venezuela the mouth of the Orinoco and control of the Orinoco basin, these being the most important questions at issue"*. Britain was awarded the less important rest. It was a success for Venezuela; the law firm used the prestigious Journal's account of the Award to adorn its credentials. They were not overweening. In the days following the Award, on 7 October 1899, Venezuela's Ambassador to Britain, Jose Andrade – the brother of the then Venezuelan President – commented: *We were given the exclusive dominion over the Orinoco, which was the principle aim we sought to achieve through arbitration.*

THE JUSTICE OF THE AWARD

"Greatly indeed did justice shine forth when, in spite of all, in the determining of the frontier the exclusive dominion of the Orinoco was granted to us, which is the principal aim which we set ourselves to obtain through arbitration. I consider well spent the humble efforts which I devoted personally to this end during the last six years of my public life."

Sr. Andrade, Venezuelan Minister to London, October 7, 1899

Two months after the Award the American President William McKinley (Venezuela's patron) confirmed the mood of satisfaction in London and Caracas – in his State of the Union Message to Congress on 5 December, 1899.

President McKinley's State of the Union Message to Congress, 5 December 1899

"The International Commission of Arbitration appointed under The Anglo-Venezuelan Treaty of 1897 rendered an award on October 3 last whereby the boundaries line between Venezuela and British Guiana is determined; thus ending a controversy which had existed for the greater part of the century. The award, as to which the Arbitrators were unanimous, while not meeting the extreme contention of either party, gives to Great Britain a large share of the interior territory in dispute and to Venezuela the entire mouth of the Orinoco, including Barima Point and the Caribbean littoral for some distance to the eastwards. The decision appears to be equally satisfactory to both parties."

Demarcation of the Boundary

AS required by the Treaty and the Award, the boundary as determined by the Award was demarcated on the ground between 1900 and 1904 by Commissioners appointed by Britain and Venezuela. For Venezuela, the Commissioners were Dr Abraham Tirado, Civil Engineer of the United States of Venezuela and Chief

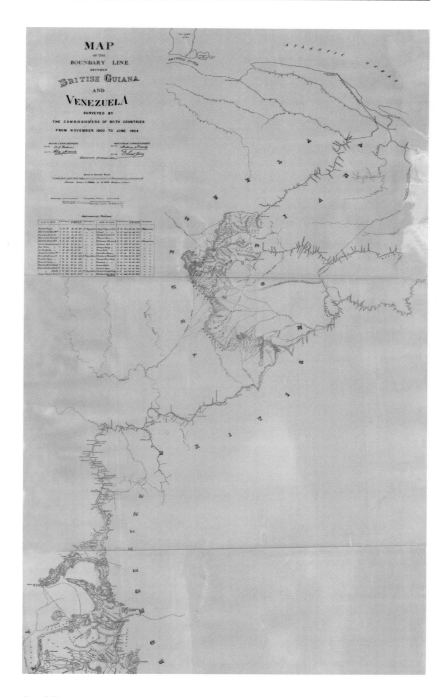

The Official Boundary Map, 1905

of the Boundary Commission and Dr Elias Toro, Surgeon General of 'the Illustrious Central University of Venezuela' and Second Commissioner on behalf of Venezuela. On 7th January 1905, an official boundary map delineating the boundary as awarded and demarcated was drawn up, signed by Dr Tirado and Dr Toro, and by the British Commissioners H.J. Perkins and C. Wilgress Anderson, and promulgated in Georgetown at the Combined Court.

The Report submitted to the Venezuelan Government by Dr Tirado, the head of the Venezuelan Boundary Commissioners, speaks volumes of Venezuelan recognition and satisfaction with the Treaty, the Award and the Map – as the closing words of his report convey.

Dr Tirado's Report Forwarding the Official Boundary Map

The honourable task is ended and the delimitation between our Republic and the Colony of British Guiana an accomplished fact.
I, satisfied with the part which it has been my lot to play, congratulate Venezuela in the person of the patriotic Administrator who rules her destinies and who sees with generous pride the long-standing and irritating dispute that has caused his country so much annoyance settled under his regime.
Abraham Tirado
March 20, 1905

Venezuela protects the Boundary

THAT this was no pretence of respect for the Award and the related delimitation was well borne out in 1911 in replacing the Marker at the northernmost point of the Boundary (Punta Playa) when it was found to be washed away. Venezuela insisted that the replacement be strictly in accord with the 1899 Paris Award. The then President of Venezuela specifically authorised the undertaking.

> ## General Juan Vicente Gomez
> ## President of the US of Venezuela
>
> **WHEREAS I confer FULL POWERS that in his capacity a Commissioner following the instructions given will proceed to replace the post which was washed away by the sea in the extreme of the frontier between Venezuela and British Guiana at Punta Playa with another which necessarily will be placed at the precise point where the boundary line cut now the line fixed in nineteen hundred in accordance with the Award signed at Paris the 3rd of October by the Mixed Commission Anglo-Venezuelan.**
> **(Sgd) J. V. Gomez**
> **Translation (sgd) Antonio G. Monagas**
> **Consul for the U.S. of Venezuela.**

It was the boundary as shown on that definitive map of 1905, authenticated with pride by their Minister of Internal Relations, F. Alientaro, that the then Venezuelan Government used to celebrate their first one hundred years of Independence in 1911. A century and five years later, as Guyana celebrates its first fifty years of its freedom, Venezuela casts that map aside – the map it celebrated in the name of Bolivar for over 60 years – to deny the new Guyana its own patrimony.

It was not always so; in 1931, for example – and there are many such instances of Venezuelan official fidelity to the 1899 Award – in the context of the tri-junction point of the boundary between Brazil, Guyana and Venezuela, Venezuela insisted on staying strictly in accord with the 1899 Award and the Official Boundary Map. To a British proposal for a minor adjustment by agreement Venezuela argued that, for constitutional reasons, they would not depart from the letter of the 1899 Award. The Venezuelan Minister of Foreign Affairs, P. Itriago Chacín wrote (in translation) on 31 October 1931 explaining their objection in principle to any change in the established border.

Venezuela rejects any change from the line of the 1899 Award
The letter from Foreign Minister Chacín

"At the present time also there exist objections of principle to an alteration by agreement to the frontier de droit, since, as this frontier is the result of a public treaty ratified by the Venezuelan legislature, it could only be modified by a process which would take considerable time even supposing that other difficulties, also of principle, could be got over."

31st October, 1931

Ten years later, into the early forties, a Venezuelan Foreign Minister, Dr Gil Borges, could reassure a British Ambassador in Caracas, D. St Clair Gainer, in the context of a press comment about the Arbitral Award, that – as the Ambassador reported him – *"From time to time an odd article about British Guiana appears in the Press but that I need take no notice of that; the articles were obviously written by persons of little knowledge who have never had access to official files. So far as the Venezuelan Government were concerned the one really satisfactory frontier Venezuela possessed (at that time) was the British Guiana frontier and it would not occur to them to dispute it.* Ambassador Gainer was reassured that the matter was *'chose jugee'*, and said so to the Minister.

How much more worthy it would have been had Venezuela continued to adopt the candidly honest stand of its Foreign Minister as late as 1941.

I will return to the sordid tale of how Venezuela abandoned the path of propriety, and with it the rule of law; and how, particularly now, its rulers seek to dispossess Guyana of its heritage and to mar the environment of our 50th anniversary.

Suriname's Questionings

INDEPENDENCE, the withdrawal of the colonial power, stirs many a dormant ambition; and so it was on our eastern border as well – from Dutch Guiana (Suriname), not yet free from Holland, but with substantial autonomy. The Netherlands and Britain had actually agreed the text of a definitive Treaty marking the boundary between Dutch and British Guiana in 1939. The outbreak of war in Europe put signature on hold, and when they returned to it after 1945, Suriname (itself now looking to Independence) had other thoughts, and tried to back away from the boundary line of the 1939 agreement. However, that is the boundary each inherited at independence. It was not the most favourable to Guyana because the vagaries of European 19th Century history had left two Dutch Governors to conclude the eastern boundary of Berbice – as folk history has it, 'over a bottle of Dutch gin' – leaving open the ownership of the Corentyne River for a later time. That was 1799. It left a legacy that was to loiter into the first and more of Guyana's fifty years of Independence.

The Boundary with Brazil

TO the south of Venezuela and to the South and South west of Guyana contiguously, is Brazil. The southernmost point of the Venezuela-Guyana border lies on the Brazilian frontier and constitutes a tri-junction international boundary point. That point was identified by the 1899 Arbitral Award and subsequently marked on the ground. It is an exotic point of conjuncture on Mount Roraima – the mountain whose flat sandstone summit Conan Doyle immortalised as the site of his lost City of Atlantis.

Venezuela's eastern boundary on the summit of Mt. Roraima

Brazil shares a boundary with every country in South America except Ecuador and Chile; and it has settled its boundaries with every single neighbour. It is a record of which Brazil is justly proud. Even in the architectural wonderland that is Brasilia, *Itamaraty,* Brazil's Foreign Ministry, is a special place, and the *Treaty Room* within it, dedicated to that achievement of frontier settlement, has an aura of sanctity. Brazil has worked hard at securing this notable achievement, and settling the border with Guyana (and with Suriname) was among those efforts.

In 1926, Brazil and Britain concluded a general boundary treaty (ratified on 16 April 1929) which "finally fixed the frontier" between them, *'from the heights of the Roraima mountains to the source of the Takutu river'* and then *"along the watershed between the Amazon basin and the basins of the Essequibo and the Corentyne, as far as the point of convergence of the frontier of the two countries, with that of Dutch Guiana, or the Colony of Suriname".*

The Joint Boundary Commission

THE next step was demarcating on the ground the actual boundary from Mt Roraima's tri-junction point with Venezuela to the Corentyne tri-junction point with Suriname. This had to be a joint exercise with British Guiana, and Brazil proposed the appointment of a Joint Boundary Commission for this purpose. Britain agreed; and this final stage in the process of border settlement was put in hand. It was to be an arduous exercise over many years through demanding terrain and with loss of life. In *The Mataruki Trail,* (published in 2006), retired Brigadier-General Joe Singh has edited the diary of one of the British surveyors – J. Arthur Hudson – who was part of that Joint Team which cut and marked on foot from point to point – some 1,119 kilometres – today's Brazil/Guyana boundary.

The Dutch join to fix the Tri-Junction Point

RECOGNISING that the tri-junction point would mark the boundary of both Brazil and Guyana with Suriname, it did not take long for the three Governments to agree that Dutch surveyors should join the Brazil-British Guiana Team for demarcating the tri-junction boundary point. In effect, they would determine and mark jointly with Guiana and Brazil the southern land boundary terminal between Guiana and Suriname at a point on their continuous border with Brazil. Separately, the Dutch and British Boundary Commissioners would continue north to determine and mark the northern land boundary terminal between Guiana and Suriname at the mouth of the Corentyne River – in effect, the beginning of their maritime boundary – then only through the 3 mile territorial sea.

The British/ Dutch/ Brazilian Boundary Commissioners determined the tri-junction point of the boundary between British Guiana,

Suriname and Brazil to be at the source of the Kutari River on the watershed with Brazil. And they marked the terminal point in the south – as the British and Dutch Commissioners were later to do in the north. A monument exists marking the tri-junction point – the southernmost point of the boundary between Guyana and Suriname. The Report on the tri-Junction Point was signed by the Heads of the three Commissions to the following effect:

The Mixed Commission, being satisfied that this is the only river which in any way answers to Schomburgk's description of the Kutari agreed that the boundary between Surinam and British Guiana, as defined in the instructions issued to the Mixed Commission, should follow the left bank of its longest branch.

The Guyana/Suriname/Brazil Tri-Junction Point, Kutari Head, January 1936

This was no surprise. As far back as 1888 an official map of the Corentyne River boundary drawn by the Government Land Surveyor in Suriname (W.L. Loth) and issued the next year with the approval of the Governor (M.L. Smidt) showed the Kutari as the Upper

Extracts from *The Mataruki Trail*

Finding the source of the Upper Courantyne/Kutari River and Fixing the Tri-junction point on the boundary of British Guiana, Suriname and Brazil

THE BRITISH/DUTCH/BRAZILIAN BOUNDARY COMMISSION

"... Metford, in the course of mapping the topography near the watershed, now discovered that there was a longer branch of East Kutari than the obvious one at which we had at first camped...

Hiscock completed his traverse up this creek, and found that it was actually the longest branch of the Kutari. A general move was therefore made to its source. Admiral Kayser made some tests of the underground water with coloured fluids, and then accepted the fact...

The area of the outcrop, was large, four or five hundred yards by a hundred or more wide, and ran down to the actual sources of the creeks on each side of the watershed. This made it a splendid landmark for the Tri-junction Point...

From its size and position there can be little doubt that this was the 'hole in the forest', which Farabee and Ogilvy had named the Farogle Rock...

My job [C. Arthur Hudson] was building the pillar... the cement ran rather short for finally fixing it up and cutting the three inscriptions. The position was agreed at Lat.1° 56' 58.2" N and Long. 56° 28' 24.5"W."

Corentyne. This definitive process notwithstanding, a contention arose in Suriname as to whether the Kutari was the appropriate continuation of the Corentyne or the 'New River' – a tributary to the west of the Corentyne. The New River had been shown on the 'Loth' map – but to the west of the Kutari and within British Guiana. If the New River was the Upper Corentyne boundary, Suriname's land area would be enlarged by some 6000 square miles. Not surprisingly, this proposition was more vigorously

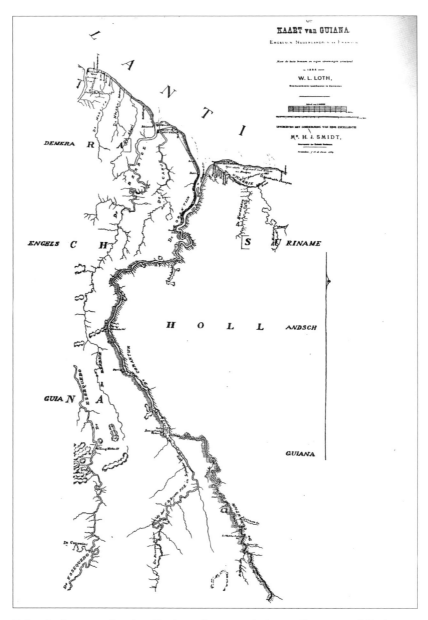

Extract of a map showing the boundary area between Guyana and Suriname, published in Holland in 1889. The inscription of the map is translated as follows: "MAP OF GUIANA. British, Dutch and French. Based on the best (available) information and my own measurements, drawn in 1888 by W.L LOTH Government Land Surveyor in Suriname. Issued with the approval of His Excellency Mr H J SMIDT, Governor of the Colony of Suriname, Amsterdam, J. H. de Bussy, 1889"

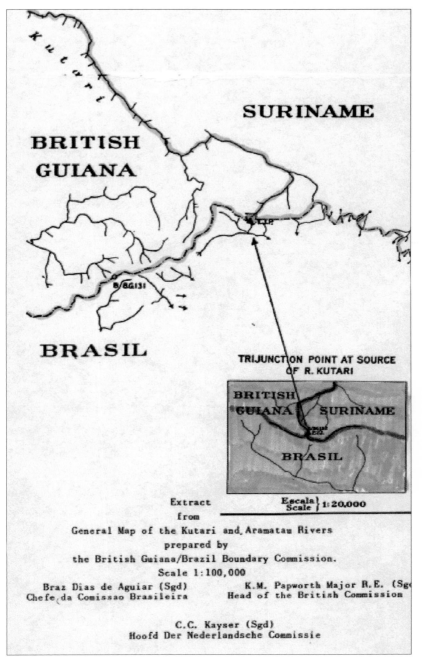

Official Map fixing the Tri Junction Point of British Guiana/Suriname/Brazil, 1936

pursued in Suriname than in the Netherlands whose Government believed the matter to be foreclosed by practice and agreement – and said so.

In an Aide Memoire of 4 August 1931 the Netherlands confirmed to Britain its agreement that *"The frontier between Suriname and British Guiana is formed by the left [i.e. west or British Guiana] bank of the Corentyne and the Cutari up to its source, which rivers are Netherlands territory."* It was on the basis of this exchange that the Netherlands, along with the United Kingdom and Brazil, embarked on the particular task of locating the source of the Kutari River and fixing the tri-junction point where the boundaries of British Guiana, Suriname and Brazil meet – the exercise so vividly described in *The Mataruki Trail.* It was with that provenance that the independent Guyana was born.

Fixing the 'Northern Terminal'

IN addition to fixing the tri-junction point at the southern extremity of the border, the British and Dutch members of the Joint Boundary Commission (without participation by their Brazilian counterpart) were instructed to establish the precise boundary point between British Guiana and Suriname at the northern end of the border. This would be at the mouth of the Corentyne River. The point was fixed in July 1936. The Boundary Commissioners established the land boundary terminus at a specific point on the west (British Guiana) side of the Corentyne River, near where the river empties into the Atlantic Ocean. The point is commonly referred to as 'Point 61' – after Village No. 61, which existed at that location. A full description of their meticulous work is set out in their *Report on the Inauguration of the Mark at the Northern Terminal of the Boundary Between Surinam and British Guiana.*

For the remainder of the colonial period – in excess of thirty years – the United Kingdom and the Netherlands treated Point 61 as the northern land boundary terminus between their respective colonies. Since their independence, Guyana in 1966 and Suriname in 1975, both expressly recognised Point 61 as the land boundary terminus. This is significant for the delimitation of the maritime boundary as this point is also the starting point for delimiting the maritime areas, and it has invariably been treated as such. It was in this manner, in 1936, that the British and Dutch Boundary Commissioners fixed the northern land boundary terminus for British Guiana and Suriname at Point 61. It was a process that would be revisited 71 years later (2007) and confirmed in every respect.

Guyana's Independence stirs Suriname

WITH the river boundary settled, the Southern tri-junction point with Brazil agreed and marked, and with the Northern maritime starting point also agreed and marked, the pre-Independent British Guiana had every right to believe its eastern border settled, including (under international law), its eastern maritime boundary with Suriname. Disappointingly, voices in Suriname (mainly local political contenders) continued to be raised in nationalist assertion of Surinamese ownership of the New River area. In other words, in denial of the validity of the tri-junction point fixed and marked at the source of the Kutari – as recently as 1936 – by the Boundary Commission, including by its Dutch member, Admiral Kayser. It was as if dormant ambition was aroused by the prospect of contending against the young newborn neighbour rather than the old but sturdy colonial power – the same bullying the infant Guyana was enduring from Venezuela to the west. And the demands were just as frenetic.

In April, 1966, the month before Guyana's Independence, Johan Adolf Pengel, then Minister-President of the not yet independent

Suriname declared: *"In view of the forthcoming independence of British Guiana the Suriname Government wishes the British to make it clear when sovereignty was transferred that the frontier was disputed"*. The British, of course, did no such thing. On 26 May 1966, the Constitution of the Independent Guyana proclaimed the boundaries of Guyana.

> ## 1966 Independence Constitution of Guyana
> ## The State and the Constitution
>
> **Art. 1. (2) The territory of Guyana shall comprise all the areas that immediately before 26th May, 1966, were comprised in the former Colony of British Guiana together with such other areas as may be declared by Act of Parliament to form part of the territory of Guyana.**

In the very first full month of Independence, in June 1966, a meeting of Guyana and Suriname officials in London allowed Guyana to assert the right of the new country to the New River area and to demonstrate how utterly indefensible would be a Suriname contention that the boundary could be otherwise than on the Kutari.

Suriname's trespass in the New River area

BY every token of history, custom, usage, prescription and recognition, indeed by every criterion of international law, Guyana's title to the New River Triangle is unassailable. But Suriname's illusion of entitlement went beyond assertion to attempted occupation. In early December 1967, within the first 18 months of Independence, the Guyana Police Force discovered a Suriname Survey Party in the New River Triangle. It re-crossed the border into Suriname when requested to leave. Guyana protested to the

Netherlands and to Suriname and the upshot was an understanding that Suriname would refrain from encroaching on Guyana's territory. However, Suriname's politicians had other ideas and began a clandestine occupation of the New River triangle in breach of the understanding arrived at in 1967.

In 1969, Guyana faced a direct challenge to its sovereignty. The Guyana Defence Force (GDF) in the course of patrolling Guyana's borders with Suriname identified an unauthorised Camp and a partly completed airstrip on Guyana territory west of the Corentyne River within the New River triangle. On 19 August, in the course of investigating the Camp, the GDF encountered a number of uniformed Surinamese – between 50 and 55. The Surinamese offered resistance to the GDF personnel for a short while before abandoning the Camp and fleeing in the direction of the Suriname border. Maps left by them revealed a plan to occupy the whole of the New River area with a series of encampments, with the Camp which the GDF had discovered serving as a base and supply headquarters. Guyana's security forces had served the young country well. One of their number, Brigadier David Granger, now Guyana's President, has chronicled the encounters with rather special authenticity.

The Defence of the New River, 1967-1969
by David A Granger (2009)

"On the defence side, it was an expensive burden for a small state like Guyana to acquire and deploy military resources to protect one long border. It was much moreso to protect two long borders. But such was the task that had to be done to make the nation safe. About forty years ago, in December 1967 and August 1969 two major police and military operations had to be undertaken to defend the New River Zone on the border with Suriname". (p.1)

Strong Notes of Protest were sent to both the Netherlands and Suriname Governments; and many efforts made by Guyana to engage Suriname in serious dialogue to no avail – despite high-level visits to Capitals and Commissions of various kinds. Worse still is the fact that Suriname's aggression in the New River triangle in Guyana's very earliest years was to be repeated much later at the other end of the Corentyne – in Guyana's maritime space.

Suriname aggression at sea

AS the 21st century dawned, the Caribbean region could have looked with satisfaction on some two centuries of the rule of law in its waters. The Caribbean Sea itself, the maritime spaces between the islands and mainland territories, were now a zone of peace. The time of European swash-buckling piracy was over – relegated to the region's folklore. Gunboat diplomacy was associated with powers external to Caribbean shores. It was in that more peaceful and settled environment that, within a programme of offshore resource development, Guyana awarded an oil exploration licence to a small Canadian Company, CGX. The concession was nothing new; its terms followed earlier licences granted by Guyana, and covered areas close to the historical equidistance line where drilling had been carried out before. Guyana had no reason to expect that activities under the CGX licence should cause any particular difficulties.

Until May 2000, some twelve months after CGX had begun its activities in the maritime area, Suriname indicated no concern or difficulty with CGX's presence in the concession area or its oil exploration activities. In that month, however, the situation changed; and for reasons that had more to do with what was happening onshore than offshore. National elections were pending in Suriname and some Opposition forces saw fit to make the CGX concession an issue in the elections, scheduled for 25 May 2000. These political forces began sharply accusing the governing Coalition of acquiescing in Guyana's petroleum exploration activities in "Surinamese" waters. Political machismo was stirring the nationalist pot.

The parliamentary elections were held in Suriname on 25 May 2000. The New Front, a coalition of four parties, won 33 of 51 parliamentary seats, defeating the incumbent National Democratic Party-led coalition. By 31 May, however, the new President of Suriname was still to be elected by the necessary two-thirds majority of parliament and political postures were still considered important in the unfolding configuration of political power.

That same day – 31 May 2000 – the defeated and, therefore, out-going Government of Suriname ordered CGX to immediately cease all activities in its concession area, and threatened adverse action if the company refused to comply. This action was taken without awaiting a reply or even leaving time for a reply. Guyana proposed a high level dialogue *"within twenty-four hours"*. That call went unheeded by Suriname. In the early morning hours of 3 June, shortly after midnight, two gunboats from the Surinamese navy arrived at the CGX concession area and circled CGX's oil rig and drill ship, the *C.E. Thornton*. The Surinamese gunboats trained their searchlights on the drilling platform, established radio contact with the *C.E. Thornton* and its accompanying service vessels, and ordered the rig to *"leave the area within twelve hours, or the consequences will be yours"*. This order was repeated several times. Crew members aboard the *C.E. Thornton* were fearful that they would be fired upon, so they detached the rig's legs from the sea floor and withdrew from the concession area hastily. The Surinamese gunboats followed, to ensure that there was no return to the area.

The rig was so seriously threatened that its U.S. owners contacted their Embassy in Georgetown, which maintained contact with the rig to ensure its safety as it withdrew from the concession area. A Surinamese aircraft buzzed overhead and naval vessels remained within striking distance throughout the rig's difficult departure. CGX did not return to the concession area in furtherance of that drilling programme because of the continuing threat from Suriname. As a result of Suriname's action, CGX incurred significant financial losses, including its investment in and the costs of the rig, service vessels and crews estimated by CGX to amount to more than US $5.5 million. The company was not prepared to risk another loss of this magnitude. Other companies, which had previously contracted to perform exploratory activities in Guyana's waters, were similarly unwilling to risk a military assault on their operations by Suriname. As a result of Suriname's aggression, Guyana itself suffered direct financial loss and foregone development opportunities; as it turned out, opportunities forgone for seven years.

There followed a period of protracted protests and counter charges, including efforts at mediation by the Prime Ministers of Trinidad and Tobago and of Jamaica; all to no avail. It became clear to Guyana that Suriname's strategy was to refuse to entertain any proposal on maritime delimitation unless Guyana ceded sovereignty over the New River Triangle to Suriname. The new President in Paramaribo could not be blamed for the resort to force; but seemed ready to take advantage of a situation his predecessor's wrong had induced – in order to wrest from Guyana what was palpably part of its patrimony.

Guyana had long considered that, given their nature, the issues concerning the maritime boundary are separate and distinct and capable of resolution without reference to unrelated matters concerning riverine or land boundaries. In particular, by the time the present dispute crystallised with Suriname's use of force in June 2000, the parties had been in agreement as to the point of origin of the maritime boundary at Point 61 for more than 60 years. From Guyana's perspective, the refusal of Suriname to resolve outstanding issues by formalising agreement on the maritime boundary was not due to any practical, technical or legal objection. Rather, it was part of a deliberate strategy to force Guyana to make concessions on unrelated issues concerning a distant land dispute that is geographically and juridically unconnected to the ocean or to maritime boundary issues. Not wholly unlike the stratagems of Venezuela.

Recourse to International Law

BY late 2003 it had become clear to Guyana that there was no prospect of resolving the distinct dispute which had arisen with Suriname over the use of force in June 2000. Guyana recognised that further attempts to negotiate a maritime boundary agreement, would be futile. The only viable option left to Guyana would be to invoke its rights under the United Nations Convention on the Law of the Sea (UNCLOS) and initiate arbitration proceedings under Part XV of the 1982 Convention. On 24 February 2004, Guyana delivered to Suriname the Notice of Arbitration and Statement of Claim under the Convention. The following day, in his Address to the Nation, President Jagdeo explained the reasons for doing so.

> *The Government of Guyana has a clear and pressing duty to seek to resolve our maritime differences with Suriname by every peaceful means. Fortunately, as the Government of Barbados has recently demonstrated in its maritime dispute with Trinidad and Tobago, such means are at hand in the form of procedures available under the United*

President Bharrat Jagdeo

Nations Convention on the Law of the Sea to which both Guyana and Suriname are parties. These procedures allow for disputes relating to maritime boundaries between adjacent States which are parties to the Treaty to be submitted for binding resolution to an Arbitral Tribunal established under the Treaty.

The proceedings were to last some three and a half years. They would end, however, in total vindication of Guyana's essential contentions; and in a firm and unambiguous finding of the illegality of Suriname's resort to force that will be of far reaching significance in the evolution of the rule of law in the world's maritime spaces including, of course, the Caribbean's – perhaps, even Guyana's. And, beyond the issue of the use of force, the Tribunal delimited the maritime boundary with Suriname on the basis of the equidistance principle, as Guyana had contended and as CGX's operations had respected.

Not without significance, in their Award, the UNCLOS Arbitral Tribunal both acknowledged and respected the 1899 Arbitral Award on the boundary with Venezuela in at least three important respects. First, in the construction of the equidistance line of the maritime boundary between Guyana and Suriname – starting on the west with Guyana's first base point at Devonshire Flats on the Essequibo Coast. Secondly, in the measurement of Guyana's coastal frontage from Waini Point in the west. Thirdly, in the inclusion, within Guyana's overall land area, of the Essequibo region – and the New River triangle. The 'shape' of Guyana as settled by the 1899 Award was affirmed.

The United Nations Convention on the Law of the Sea has a history entwined with Guyana which has long felt a special commitment to its highest purposes. In a modest way, as a small developing country, Guyana has always identified fully with those purposes.

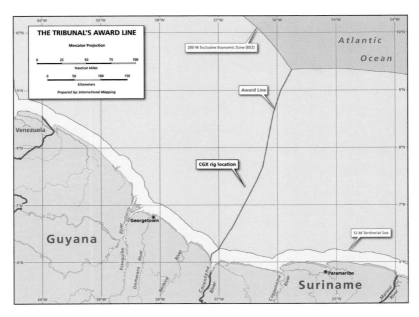

The Guyana-Suriname Maritime Boundary

Guyana has always been proud of the fact that it was its ratification of the Treaty, the 60th, in 1993, that brought the Convention into force.

Venezuelan greed revived

GUYANA'S controversies with Venezuela have always had a sharper edge than those with Suriname, perhaps because the former derive to a greater degree from cultivated avarice and calculated stratagems –all sustained by awareness of unequal strengths. These are not attributes of the Venezuelan people; they dwell within coteries of Venezuelan power, both civilian and military; and they are self-sustaining, feeding on their co-mingled myths and ambitions, and generating new falsehoods which they begin to believe. For sixty years Venezuelan Governments respected, adopted, even protected the 1899 boundary; yet today President Maduro can say in a studied distortion of history: *With the 20th Century came the third stage. The Treaty of Paris was denounced as invalid.* By 'the Treaty of Paris' he means the Arbitral Tribunal that met in Paris and the Award of 1899 and the demarcated boundary that Venezuela respected for sixty years of that 20th century – another distortion on which is being built another stratagem of dispossession: one that may have as much to do with Venezuela's internal political maelstrom as Guyana-Venezuela relations.

So, now, as Guyana looks to marking with pride the 50th Anniversary of its Independence, the settlement of its border with Venezuela, secured by the 1899 Arbitral Award and its formal demarcation, is being brusquely threatened by forces in Caracas – in furtherance of earlier efforts to subvert the rules of international law and virtually steal Guyana's substance.

Satisfied initially with its achievements under the 1899 Award, though not without the grumbles of the greedy who wanted even more, Venezuela proceeded toward fulfilment of the destiny which the vast mineral wealth of its land yielded – including from the Orinoco Basin that the Award gave them; and without which that region would be in contention. Through most of the first half of the 20th century it found no quarrel with the Award; and when in 1962 it chose to reopen it with Britain – some 60 years after it had insistently closed it – it did so with restraint and circumspection in the manner of equals. But time was on the side of those in Venezuela for whom, with national wealth now assured, eastward expansion had become an imperial crusade. And the ground was well prepared.

The Mallet-Prevost stratagem

AT the first sign of Guyana's movement to independence, the Venezuelan Government initiated a vigorous boundary controversy on the most tenuous of grounds. The single source of these grounds was, and remains to this day, a memorandum written by an American lawyer, Severo Mallet-Prevost, who was one of the junior counsel for Venezuela during the Arbitral Tribunal's hearing. It was written in 1944 just after he had received from the Government of Venezuela the Order of the Liberator for his services to the Republic. But the slanderous tale was not told then. It was embedded in a secret memorandum given to his law partner in Washington with strict instructions to be opened and published only after his death. He died in 1949 – when every other participant in the arbitral proceedings had long since died. The posthumous memorandum contended that the Arbitral Award of 1899 was the result of a political deal between Britain and Russia carried into effect by collusion between the British Judges and the Russian President of the Tribunal and agreed to in the interest of unanimity by the American Judges – after they had consulted with the American lawyers (including himself) who were Venezuela's chosen counsel.

It was on this flimsiest pretext of an old and disappointed man's posthumous memoirs set down some 45 years after the events – these shreds and patches embroidered with speculations, ambiguities and allusions to new but undisclosed evidence; these calumnies against five of the most eminent jurists in the world of their time – that Venezuela mounted its international campaign against Guyana as we approached independence. As the date drew nearer the agitation grew fiercer threatening in veiled and indirect ways the advance to Independence itself. Hence the British conversations in Geneva in 1966 – three months before Guyana's Independence.

The 'Cold War' dimension

BUT there was more, until now, hidden in archival secrecy. Though long suspected, American State Papers (both White House and State Department Papers since declassified) have now revealed a darker plot. In the 1950s and 1960s, in a 'cold war' context, there was serious Western concern, mainly driven by the United States, that Guyana's independence under a Jagan-led Government would see another Cuba, this time on the South American Continent. In 1962, the then Venezuelan President Rómulo Betancourt chose to take advantage of this fear of 'another Cuba' in an independent Guyana by proposing a plan to develop the Essequibo region by US and British investors no longer as part of British Guiana – but under 'Venezuelan sovereignty' – a pretext for intervention and acquisition under the guise of curbing the spread of' 'communism'.

A despatch of 15 May 1962 from the American Ambassador in Caracas (C. Allan Stewart) conveyed to the State Department Betancourt's views on the "border question" as gleaned "during the course of several meetings" with him. He wrote with the astuteness of a seasoned diplomat:

> *"President Betancourt professes to be greatly concerned about an independent British Guiana with Cheddie Jagan as Prime Minister. He suspects that Jagan is already too committed to communism and that his American wife exercises considerable influence over him... This alarm may be slightly simulated since Betancourt's solution of the border dispute presupposes a hostile Jagan.*

> *"His plan: Through a series of conferences with the British before Guiana is awarded independence a* cordon sanitaire *would be set up between the present boundary line and one mutually agreed upon by the two countries (Venezuela and Britain). Sovereignty of this slice of British Guiana would pass to Venezuela. ...*

> *"Of course, the reason for the existence of the strip of territory, according to the President, is the danger of communist infiltration of Venezuela from British Guiana if a Castro-type government ever were established... It would seem logical that Venezuela will from now on pursue the idea of the cordon sanitaire to protect itself from a commie-line independent British Guiana rather than send support to the Burnham opposition."*

A year later, on 30 June 1963, President Kennedy was meeting Britain's Prime Minister Macmillan at Birch Grove in England and, on the American side, the issue of British Guiana was the *"principal* subject the President intend(ed) to raise with Macmillan". So wrote Dean Rusk (the American Secretary of State) the week before in a secret telegram to Ambassador Bruce (the U.S. Ambassador in London) seeking his thoughts "on how best to convince our British friends of the deadly seriousness of our concern and our determination that British Guiana shall not become independent with a Communist government." The commonality of motivation between Kennedy and Betancourt was quite remarkable. Much more remarkable is the inheritance, adoption and vigorous pursuit of an abandoned CIA legacy by an avowed, radical, anti-imperialist Venezuelan Government of the present – and in the name of Bolivar.

Of course, none of this was ever revealed to the Venezuelan people whose patriotism was infused with the simplistic fallacy that Venezuela was 'robbed' by Britain of the Essequibo region of Guyana. On their maps, and in their minds, it was the 'Zona en Reclamation'. As it was, it was Jagan's political opponent, Burnham, who led the Independent Guyana. But by then, driven by Venezuela's greed, the 'controversy' had taken on a life of its own, certainly for the chauvinistic forces that had nurtured it. For those forces the Mallet-Prevost fable would suffice to perpetuate the contention that the 1899 Arbitral Award is 'null and void' and the Essequibo region automatically Venezuelan, studiously ignoring the implications of the nullity contention for the Orinoco Delta which the same Award had given to them. That was and is today Venezuela's basic contention – that the 1899 Arbitral Award is 'null and void' because of the Mallet-Prevost posthumous memoire.

The 'David and Goliath' torment

THE young, and powerless, Guyana faced this 'David and Goliath' situation, and its attendant harassment, from birth. Its only defence was diplomacy: an appeal to the international community to save the infant state from the machinations of its large, wealthy, powerful – and alas, unscrupulous – neighbour. And in those days, Venezuela pursued its territorial ambitions shamelessly. It kept Guyana out of the Organisation of American States (OAS) until 1991 and, within months of independence, it brazenly breached the border (on Ankoko Island) in defiance of the Geneva Agreement. The same year it began interfering in Guyana's internal affairs through attempted subversion of Guyana's indigenous people. In 1968, as Guyana's Prime Minister paid an official visit to Britain, Venezuela bought advertising space in the London *Times* (of 15 June), announcing its non-recognition of concessions granted by Guyana in the area it 'claimed'. Later that year, contemptuous of international law, President Leoni issued a 'decree' purporting to annex a strip of territorial waters adjacent to Guyana's coast. It refused, of course, to sign the Law of the Sea Convention – one of the few countries in the world to exclude itself from '*the Constitution for the Oceans*'. The young Guyana faced fearful odds. Surmounting them became Guyana's mission in the world.

Speaking for Guyana in the General Debate of the 23rd session of the United Nations General Assembly (on 3 October 1968), I devoted my entire Address to the issue of Venezuela's attempts to stifle Guyana at birth. I called it: "*Development or Defence: the Small State threatened with Aggression*'. It was to continue to be an apt description of Guyana's predicament throughout the fifty years of its existence.

I have earlier indicated how, in rejecting Venezuela's devious attempts to defer Guyana's Independence, Britain sought to rid the new Guyana of the Venezuelan 'plague'. February 17th, 2016 was the 50th anniversary of the signing of the 1966 Geneva Agreement. It is not co-incidental that 2016 is also the 50th Anniversary of Guyana's Independence; for the Geneva Meeting represented the last effort from Caracas to prevent Guyana's Independence.

The Geneva Agreement, 1966

THE Agreement was between Britain and Venezuela; Guyana only became a party on attaining Independence. And that is what it was essentially about – Guyana's Independence. Until then, Venezuela had indulged an argument with Britain that Bolivar's legacy could never have blessed, namely, to retain the status of colonialism in British Guiana until the boundary with Venezuela was changed. The Geneva Agreement ended that un-Bolivarian argument. Guyana would be free with its borders intact. That is why Guyana believed the Geneva Agreement was worth commemorating; and it said so. It is part of the founding instruments of Guyana's freedom.

In that context, the Agreement carefully identified the nature of Venezuela's on-going controversy with Britain as "the controversy between Venezuela and the United Kingdom which has arisen as a result of the Venezuelan contention that the arbitral award of 1899 about the frontier between British Guiana and Venezuela is null and void." It was with this controversy that the Geneva "conversations", and their outcome in the form of the Geneva Agreement, was concerned. Having identified the controversy as that raised by Venezuela's contention of nullity of the 1899 Arbitral Award, the Geneva Agreement went on to stipulate the means which the Parties agreed must be followed to resolve the controversy.

It provided a clear path to settlement ending in judicial process. First, there would be a 4-year Mixed Commission of Guyanese and Venezuelan representatives, and if the Commission could not settle the matter and the Governments could not agree on the next means of doing so, the United Nations Secretary General would be the arbiter of the "means of settlement" from those set out in Article 33 of the Charter of the United Nations. U Thant was the UN Secretary General in 1966 and on receipt of the Agreement he replied on 4 April 1966 without equivocation.

United Nations Secretary-General's acceptance of obligations under the Geneva Agreement H.E. U Thant, 4 April 1966 to the Foreign Minister of Venezuela

"I have made note of the obligations that eventually can fall on the Secretary General of the United Nations by virtue of Paragraph 2 of Article IV of the Agreement and it pleases me to inform you that the functions are of such a nature that they can be appropriately carried out by the Secretary General of the United Nations."

The Mixed Commission did not succeed in resolving the controversy. Guyana's Representatives were Sir Donald Jackson (a former Chief Justice of British Guiana) and Dr Mohammed Shahabudeen (later, a Judge of the ICJ). The Commission held many meetings during their 4-year existence. At the very first meeting Guyana invited Venezuela to produce its evidence and arguments in support of its claim that the Arbitral Award was 'null and void'. Venezuela's response was that the issue of 'nullity' was not an issue with which the Mixed Commission should concern itself. The only issue before the Commission was how much of the Essequibo region was Guyana prepared to cede either directly or within the framework of a 'Joint Development' programme. The minutes of the Meetings of the Mixed Commission were carefully recorded and signed with copies attached to the Final Report and Interim Reports were issued to both Governments signed by the Commissioners.

In declining to address their basic legal contention of nullity in the Mixed Commission, the Venezuelan Commissioners did concede that the question of judicial settlement could arise at a later time. *'The juridical examination of the question* (of nullity) *would, if necessary, be proceeded with, in time, by some international tribunal in accordance with article IV of the Geneva Agreement'.* So said Venezuela at the end of 1966 – in the First Interim Report signed in Caracas by the Venezuelan Commissioners Luis Loreto and G Garcia Bustillos. Today, fifty years later, Venezuela still argues that that later time has not yet come.

Fifty years of Venezuelan 'filibuster'

BUT the Mixed Commission's failure to find a resolution to the controversy was due as much to what was said in the Commission as to what was done by Venezuela beyond the discussions. I have alluded to some of them above, namely, Venezuela's:

- Violation of Guyana's territorial integrity on Ankoko Island
- The Leoni attempt to appropriate Guyana's off-shore waters
- Economic aggression through campaigns against investment in Guyana
- Intervention in Guyana's internal affairs through the Rupununi 'uprising'.

And there were others. What the experience of the Mixed Commission revealed was a strategy which Venezuela has pursued for over fifty years, namely: a façade of peaceful but fruitless discussion masking a policy of studied political, economic and increasingly militaristic aggression. When the Geneva meeting was held in 1966, the expectation was a process of some 10 years to solution. Under the Protocol of Port of Spain, a moratorium of 12 years followed the Mixed Commission, but Venezuela found it too cramping of its strategy and refused to extend it. Then followed twenty-seven years of a UN 'good offices' process which yielded nothing by way of solution but suited Venezuela's strategy of continuous belligerence. With the untimely death of the last Personal Representative of the Secretary General under that process, the much respected Dr Norman Girvan, Guyana has indicated that the process has run its course. In the year of the 50th anniversary of the Geneva Agreement, and of Guyana's Independence which it heralded, it is palpably time to bring this unworthy controversy to an end.

Yet Venezuela ensures that it remains a matter of contention, though not surprisingly (given President Betancourt's' manoeuvres) less rancorous in the time of Hugo Chavez than in earlier years. However, beyond Chavez, his successor President

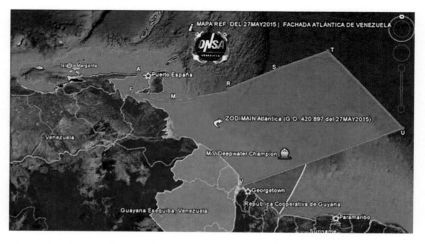

The Maduro Decree No. 1.787

Nicolás Maduro, whatever the internal political pressures, has carried Venezuela's campaign of usurpation to even more outrageous lengths – threatening both the maritime and territorial integrity of Guyana – and reaching beyond Guyana, to the maritime space of other Caribbean Community countries.

A clear path to 'judicial settlement'

IN September 2015, Guyana's new President, David Granger, called upon the Secretary General of the United Nations, Ban Ki-moon, to have Venezuela's contention that the Arbitral Award of 1899 is 'null and void' settled with finality by judicial process, under the Geneva Agreement. It is a legal contention and eminently suitable to resolution by the world's highest juridical body. The Secretary General is now seized of the matter.

Meanwhile, Venezuela's hostility persists. As recently as 4 February 2016 the Foreign Minister of Venezuela, Delcy Rodríguez, chose the precincts of the United Nations to issue a statement under the title 'Venezuela ratifies its rights over the Essequibo at the UN'. On February 11, 2016 Guyana's Vice-President and Foreign Minister, Carl Greenidge made a statement of repudiation in Guyana's National Assembly. He ended it as follows:

> *The people of Venezuela are our sisters and brothers and Guyana holds out the hand of friendship to them. But there are forces in Venezuela who have made it their life's mission, abusing the hallowed memory of Bolivar. To hold Guyana hostage to their crusade of greed.*

> *Guyana is a child of decolonisation. Its ancestry lies in the Charter of the United Nations – its purposes and*

(L-R) President of Venezuela, Nicolás Maduro, United Nations Secretary General, Ban Ki-moon, and President of Guyana, David Granger   Don Emmert/AFP/Getty Images

principles. Guyana's sovereignty and territorial integrity are its international heritage. We will ever remain faithful to the demands of both; and we look to the international community to stand with us in Venezuela's assaults upon them.

All Governments in Guyana have faced these predatory challenges over the first fifty years of Independence: all Prime Ministers, all Presidents, all political parties, all the people of Guyana. And they have faced them in solidarity. The Opposition in Guyana's Parliament today is part of the country's advisory body on 'border' issues. And so has it been before. It is essential that it so continues. A united Guyana can be confident that we shall overcome these challenges on all fronts. Our neighbours must know that they challenge a united Guyana. They must hear ringing across our borders the *Song of the Republic* sung with clear voice and from stout hearts:

From Pakaraima's peaks of pow'r
To Courantyne's lush sands,
Her children pledge each faithful hour
To guard Guyana's lands.
To foil the shock of rude invader
Who'd violate her earth,
To cherish and defend forever
The State that gave them birth.

This is a reproduction of the enhanced section of the Official Map of 1936 adopted by the British/Dutch/Brazilian Commission identifying the utmost reaches of the Kutari River on the watershed with Brazil as the source of 'de Corentjin', and marking it as the tri-junction point of the boundary of British Guiana, Suriname and Brazil.